Discover Slovenia

AVERY B. HODGES

Published by AVERY B. HODGES, 2023.

While every precaution has been taken in the preparation of this book, the publisher assumes no responsibility for errors or omissions, or for damages resulting from the use of the information contained herein.

DISCOVER SLOVENIA

First edition. October 6, 2023.

ISBN: 979-8223890072

Written by AVERY B. HODGES.

Table of Contents

Chapter 1: Introduction to Slovenia

Welcome to Slovenia, a hidden gem nestled in the heart of Europe! This chapter will provide you with a brief but comprehensive overview of this enchanting country, including its geography, history, culture, and attractions. Prepare to be captivated by the natural beauty, rich heritage, and warm hospitality that Slovenia has to offer.

Geography:

Slovenia, covering an area of approximately 20,273 square kilometers, is a small country located in Central Europe. Bordered by Italy to the west, Austria to the north, Hungary to the northeast, and Croatia to the south and southeast, Slovenia is blessed with diverse landscapes. From the stunning Julian Alps in the northwest to the idyllic coastal region along the Adriatic Sea, and from the picturesque Lake Bled to the enchanting underground caves of Postojna, Slovenia boasts a remarkable variety of natural wonders.

History:

With a history dating back to the Roman era, Slovenia has been at the crossroads of various cultures and civilizations. From the Slavic tribes that settled here in the 6th century to the Habsburg monarchy and the Yugoslav era, Slovenia has experienced a rich tapestry of influences. In 1991, Slovenia gained independence, marking a new chapter in its history as a sovereign nation. Today, it stands proudly as a member of the European Union and NATO, embracing its heritage while looking towards the future.

Culture:

Slovenia's culture is a vibrant blend of influences from its neighboring countries, yet it retains a unique identity of its own. Slovenians are known for their warm hospitality, genuine friendliness, and love for their homeland. The country's rich cultural heritage is evident in its traditional festivals, music, dance, and cuisine. From the charming capital city of Ljubljana, with its picturesque old town and vibrant arts scene, to the quaint villages that dot the countryside, Slovenia offers a captivating glimpse into its cultural tapestry.

Attractions:

Slovenia is a true playground for nature lovers and adventure enthusiasts. Whether you enjoy hiking, skiing, cycling, or simply immersing yourself in the tranquility of nature, Slovenia has something for everyone. Discover the breathtaking beauty of Triglav National Park, home to the country's highest peak and a haven for outdoor activities. Explore the mystical underground world of the Postojna Cave, adorned with stunning stalactites and stalagmites. Indulge in the charm of Lake Bled, with its fairytale-like island and medieval castle. And don't forget to experience the coastal allure of Piran, a picturesque town with narrow streets and Venetian architecture.

As you embark on your journey through Slovenia, be prepared to be captivated by the country's natural wonders, enchanted by its rich history, and embraced by its warm and welcoming culture. This is just a glimpse of what awaits you in this captivating land. So, pack your bags, open your heart, and get ready to uncover the hidden treasures of Slovenia.

Disclaimer: This chapter is intended to provide a general overview of Slovenia and its attractions. For detailed and up-to-date information, please refer to official tourism websites.

Chapter 2: When to Visit Slovenia

Slovenia, a hidden gem nestled in the heart of Europe, offers a diverse range of experiences throughout the year. From charming medieval towns to breathtaking alpine landscapes, this enchanting country has something to offer every traveler. When planning your visit to Slovenia, it is essential to consider the best time to explore its wonders. In this chapter, we will provide you with valuable tips to help you decide when to embark on your unforgettable Slovenian adventure.

1. Spring: Embrace Nature's Rebirth

As winter bids its farewell, Slovenia awakens with a burst of vibrant colors and renewed life. Spring, from April to June, is an ideal time for nature enthusiasts to visit. The countryside is adorned with blooming flowers, and the picturesque landscapes come alive. Explore the Triglav National Park, hike through the Julian Alps, or witness the awe-inspiring beauty of Lake Bled as the surrounding meadows burst into full bloom.

2. Summer: Bask in the Warmth

Slovenia truly shines during the summer months, from June to August, when the weather is warm and inviting. The sun-drenched coastline along the Adriatic Sea beckons beach lovers, offering a perfect escape for swimming, sunbathing, and indulging in delicious seafood. Additionally, this season is ideal for exploring Slovenia's charming capital, Ljubljana, with its lively outdoor cafes and cultural festivals.

3. Autumn: A Symphony of Colors

As the summer heat gradually fades, Slovenia transforms into a breathtaking tapestry of autumn hues. From September to November, the country's forests and vineyards become a painter's palette of reds, oranges, and golds. Experience the magic of the wine regions, such as Maribor and Brda, during the grape harvest season. Don't miss the traditional grape festivals, where you can sample exquisite local wines and immerse yourself in Slovenian culture.

4. Winter: A Winter Wonderland

For those seeking a fairytale winter experience, Slovenia is a true winter wonderland. From December to February, the snow-covered landscapes offer endless opportunities for skiing, snowboarding, and other winter sports. The Julian Alps boast world-class ski resorts, including Kranjska Gora and Vogel, where you can carve your way through pristine slopes. After a day on the mountains, warm up with a cup of mulled wine and indulge in hearty traditional Slovenian cuisine.

5. Festivals and Events: A Year-Round Celebration

Regardless of the season you choose to visit Slovenia, you will have the opportunity to immerse yourself in its vibrant cultural events and festivals. From the Dragon Carnival in Ptuj to the Ljubljana Summer Festival, the country's calendar is filled with celebrations that showcase its rich heritage and traditions. Be sure to check the local event listings to enhance your visit with these unique experiences.

When planning your trip to Slovenia, consider your personal preferences and desired activities. Each season offers its own unique charm, allowing you to tailor your visit to your interests. Whether you are captivated by the bloom of spring, the warmth of summer, the colors of autumn, or the enchantment of winter, Slovenia will undoubtedly leave you with unforgettable memories.

Remember, the best time to visit Slovenia ultimately depends on your preferences and the experiences you seek. By considering the information provided in this chapter, you will be well-equipped to plan your journey and make the most of your time in this captivating country.

Chapter 3: What to Pack for Your Trip to Slovenia

As you prepare for your exciting adventure to Slovenia, it's essential to pack wisely to ensure a comfortable and enjoyable trip. This chapter will guide you through the necessary items to bring along, ensuring you have everything you need for a memorable experience in this beautiful country.

1. Clothing:

Slovenia's climate varies throughout the year, so it's important to pack accordingly. During the summer months (June to August), lightweight and breathable clothing is recommended, including t-shirts, shorts, and sundresses. Don't forget to pack a swimsuit if you plan to visit the stunning lakes or coastal areas. In spring and autumn (April to May and September to October), it's advisable to bring a mix of warm and cool clothing, such as long-sleeved shirts, light jackets, and jeans. Winter months (November to March) require warm clothing, including heavy coats, sweaters, hats, gloves, and boots, as temperatures can drop significantly.

2. Footwear:

Comfortable walking shoes are a must for exploring Slovenia's charming cities and natural wonders. Whether you're strolling through Ljubljana's cobblestone streets or hiking in Triglav National Park, having sturdy and supportive footwear will ensure you can fully enjoy your adventures. Additionally, pack a pair of sandals or flip-flops for relaxing by the beach or visiting thermal spas.

3. Outdoor Gear:

If you plan to explore Slovenia's breathtaking landscapes, consider packing some outdoor gear. A lightweight backpack is essential for day trips, allowing you to carry water, snacks, and extra layers. Don't forget to bring a hat, sunglasses, and sunscreen to protect yourself from the sun's rays. Depending on your activities, you might also want to pack a rain jacket, hiking boots, and trekking poles.

4. Electronics and Adapters:

To capture the picturesque scenery and stay connected, bring along your camera or smartphone. Slovenia uses the Europlug (Type C) and Schuko (Type F) electrical outlets, so make sure to pack the appropriate adapters for your electronics.

5. Travel Documents:

Ensure you have all the necessary travel documents, including your passport, visa (if required), and travel insurance information. It's also advisable to carry a photocopy of your passport and other essential documents in case of loss or theft. Additionally, keep a printed or digital copy of your accommodation reservations, flight tickets, and any other relevant travel bookings.

6. Medications and First Aid:

If you take prescription medications, be sure to pack an adequate supply for the duration of your trip. It's also wise to bring a small first aid kit containing essentials like band-aids, pain relievers, and any personal medications you may need. Familiarize yourself with the local emergency numbers and addresses of nearby medical facilities.

7. Miscellaneous Items:

To make your trip more comfortable, consider packing a few additional items. A reusable water bottle will come in handy during your explorations, as Slovenia has many pristine water sources. A power bank will ensure your electronic devices stay charged on the go. Finally, a phrasebook or language translation app can be useful for communicating with locals who may not speak English.

Remember, packing light is always a good idea, so prioritize the essentials and leave room for any souvenirs you may want to bring back home. By following these guidelines, you'll be well-prepared for your Slovenian adventure, allowing you to fully immerse yourself in the country's rich culture, stunning landscapes, and warm hospitality.

Chapter 4: Geography and Climate of Slovenia

Introduction:

Welcome to Chapter 4 of our tourist guide to Slovenia! In this chapter, we will explore the captivating geography and climate of this beautiful country. From its majestic mountains and pristine lakes to its enchanting coastline, Slovenia offers a diverse range of landscapes that are sure to leave you in awe. So, let's embark on this journey and discover the natural wonders that await you in Slovenia!

1. Mountains:

Slovenia is renowned for its breathtaking mountain ranges, which cover a significant portion of the country. The Julian Alps dominate the northwestern region, with Triglav, the highest peak in Slovenia, standing proudly at 2,864 meters. These majestic mountains provide endless opportunities for outdoor activities, including hiking, climbing, and skiing. As you explore this alpine wonderland, prepare to be captivated by the stunning vistas and the serenity of nature.

2. Rivers:

Slovenia is crisscrossed by numerous rivers, each contributing to the country's unique charm. The emerald-green Soča River, often referred to as the Emerald Beauty is a true gem of Slovenia. Flowing through the Julian Alps, it offers breathtaking views and is a paradise for water sports enthusiasts. The picturesque Ljubljanica River, which winds its way through the heart of the capital city, Ljubljana, adds to the city's romantic atmosphere. Take a leisurely boat ride along its tranquil waters and soak in the beauty of the surrounding architecture.

3. Lakes:

Slovenia boasts an abundance of crystal-clear lakes that are nothing short of enchanting. Lake Bled, with its iconic island and medieval castle perched atop a hill, is a postcard-perfect destination. Take a leisurely stroll along the lake's edge or rent a traditional pletna boat to reach the island and ring the wishing bell. Lake Bohinj, nestled in the Triglav National Park, offers a peaceful retreat surrounded by untouched nature. Embrace the tranquility as you take a refreshing swim or embark on a kayaking adventure.

4. Coastline:

Although Slovenia may have a small coastline, it is undoubtedly a hidden gem of the Adriatic Sea. The charming town of Piran, with its Venetian architecture and narrow streets, is a coastal delight. Explore its historic center, indulge in delicious seafood, and bask in the Mediterranean ambiance. Portorož, known for its thermal spas and vibrant nightlife, offers a perfect blend of relaxation and entertainment. Unwind on its sandy beaches or try your luck at the glamorous Grand Casino.

5. Climate:

Slovenia experiences a diverse climate due to its geographical location. In the coastal region, you can expect a Mediterranean climate with hot summers and mild winters. As you venture inland, the climate becomes more continental, with warm summers and cold winters. The Alpine region experiences colder temperatures and heavier snowfall, making it a haven for winter sports enthusiasts. Regardless of the season, Slovenia's climate ensures a delightful experience for every visitor.

Conclusion:

As we conclude Chapter 4, we hope you now have a deeper understanding of Slovenia's geography and climate. From the awe-inspiring mountains and winding rivers to the captivating lakes and enchanting coastline, Slovenia offers a diverse range of natural wonders that will leave you spellbound. So, pack your bags, embrace the beauty of this country, and prepare to create unforgettable memories in Slovenia's breathtaking landscapes.

Chapter 5: The Regions of Slovenia

Introduction:

Slovenia, a small yet diverse country nestled in the heart of Europe, is known for its breathtaking landscapes, rich cultural heritage, and warm hospitality. In this chapter, we will explore the different regions of Slovenia, each with its unique characteristics and attractions. From the Julian Alps to the Adriatic Coast, Slovenia offers a diverse range of experiences that will captivate every traveler.

1. Alpine Slovenia:

Situated in the northwestern part of the country, Alpine Slovenia is a region renowned for its majestic mountains, crystal-clear lakes, and charming alpine villages. The Julian Alps dominate this area, offering a paradise for outdoor enthusiasts. Adventure seekers can indulge in activities like hiking, skiing, and mountaineering in the Triglav National Park, home to Slovenia's highest peak, Mount Triglav. Bled, with its iconic lake and medieval castle, is a must-visit destination that exudes tranquility and natural beauty.

2. Mediterranean and Karst Slovenia:

Moving towards the southwest, we enter the region of Mediterranean and Karst Slovenia, where the Adriatic Sea meets the rugged Karst landscape. The coastal towns of Piran, Portorož, and Izola showcase a unique blend of Venetian and Mediterranean architecture, offering picturesque views and a vibrant seaside atmosphere. The Škocjan Caves, a UNESCO World Heritage Site, reveal an underground world of stunning stalactites and stalagmites, leaving visitors in awe of nature's wonders.

3. Thermal Pannonian Slovenia:

Heading east, we discover the Thermal Pannonian Slovenia, a region known for its soothing thermal spas, lush vineyards, and charming rural landscapes. The town of Ptuj, with its medieval castle and vibrant carnival traditions, is a cultural gem that takes visitors on a journey through time. Wine enthusiasts can explore the vineyards of Jeruzalem and taste the region's renowned white wines, while the town of Moravske Toplice invites relaxation in its thermal waters.

4. Ljubljana and Central Slovenia:

In the heart of the country lies Ljubljana, the vibrant capital of Slovenia, surrounded by the diverse landscapes of Central Slovenia. Ljubljana's charming old town, with its colorful buildings and lively riverside cafes, offers a perfect blend of history and modernity. The region's natural beauty can be explored in the stunning Škofja Loka, Kamnik, and Velika Planina, where picturesque landscapes and traditional architecture create a captivating atmosphere.

5. Prekmurje and Pomurje:

The northeastern region of Slovenia, Prekmurje and Pomurje, is a land of vast plains, picturesque hills, and traditional rural life. The unique dialect and cultural heritage of this region set it apart from the rest of Slovenia. Visitors can experience the traditional way of life by visiting the open-air museum in Rogatec or indulging in the local delicacies, such as the famous Prekmurska gibanica, a delicious layered pastry.

Conclusion:

Slovenia's diverse regions offer a tapestry of experiences, from the stunning alpine landscapes of Alpine Slovenia to the charming coastal towns of Mediterranean and Karst Slovenia. The thermal spas of Thermal Pannonian Slovenia provide relaxation, while Ljubljana and Central Slovenia offer a vibrant urban experience. Prekmurje and Pomurje invite visitors to immerse themselves in traditional rural life. Whatever your preference, Slovenia's regions promise an unforgettable journey filled with natural beauty, cultural heritage, and warm hospitality.

Chapter 6: History and Culture of Slovenia

Introduction:

Welcome to Chapter 6 of our tourist guide, where we will take you on a journey through the rich history and vibrant culture of Slovenia. From its earliest inhabitants to the present day, Slovenia has witnessed significant events and embraced diverse influences that have shaped its unique identity. Join us as we uncover the key historical moments, prominent figures, and remarkable sites that have contributed to the country's rich heritage.

1. The Early Inhabitants:

Slovenia's history can be traced back to the prehistoric era when various tribes and cultures inhabited the region. Archaeological findings suggest that humans settled in present-day Slovenia as early as the Paleolithic era. The Illyrians, Celts, and Romans also left their mark on the land, introducing their customs and traditions.

2. The Arrival of the Slavs:

In the 6th century, the Slavs migrated to the region, establishing the foundations of Slovenian culture. Their arrival marked the beginning of the Slovenian ethnic identity, language, and cultural practices that continue to thrive today. The Slavic influence also brought forth a sense of unity among the Slovenian people.

3. The Formation of the Slovenian State:

During the Middle Ages, Slovenia was divided into several feudal states, each ruled by its own noble family. However, in the 10th century, the Slovenian territories were united under the Holy Roman Empire. This period saw the emergence of important historical figures such as the Carniolan dukes, who played a pivotal role in shaping the Slovenian state.

4. The Slovenian Reformation:

In the 16th century, Slovenia became a significant center of the Protestant Reformation. The teachings of Martin Luther and other reformers spread rapidly, leading to a transformation of religious practices in the region. The Slovenian language also gained prominence during this period, as translations of religious texts were made accessible to the common people.

5. The Habsburg Rule and Austro-Hungarian Empire:

In the 18th century, Slovenia came under the rule of the Habsburg monarchy, which later became part of the Austro-Hungarian Empire. This period witnessed the rise of the Slovenian national awakening, with notable figures such as France Prešeren, a renowned poet who became a symbol of Slovenian cultural identity.

6. World War I and the Formation of Yugoslavia:

The aftermath of World War I brought about significant changes in the region. Slovenia, along with other South Slavic territories, formed the Kingdom of Serbs, Croats, and Slovenes, which later became the Kingdom of Yugoslavia. Despite political challenges, Slovenia's cultural and artistic scene flourished during this time.

7. World War II and Communist Era:

During World War II, Slovenia was occupied by Nazi Germany and later became part of the Socialist Federal Republic of Yugoslavia under communist rule. The post-war period saw Slovenia's gradual shift towards increased autonomy and a growing desire for independence.

8. Independence and the Modern Era:

In 1991, Slovenia declared its independence from Yugoslavia, marking a significant turning point in its history. The country swiftly transitioned into a democratic state and embraced market-oriented reforms. Today, Slovenia thrives as a member of the European Union, preserving its rich cultural heritage while embracing modernity.

Key Historical Figures and Sites:

- France Prešeren: Considered Slovenia's greatest poet, his works played a crucial role in shaping the Slovenian language and national identity.

- Ljubljana Castle: A symbol of the city's history, the castle offers panoramic views and showcases exhibitions on Slovenian history.

- Ptuj Castle: One of the oldest castles in Slovenia, it houses a museum that provides insights into the country's medieval past.

- Skocjan Caves: A UNESCO World Heritage site, these caves boast stunning natural formations and offer a glimpse into Slovenia's geological history.

Conclusion:

As we conclude Chapter 6, we hope you have gained a deeper understanding of Slovenia's captivating history and vibrant culture. From its early inhabitants to its journey towards independence, Slovenia's rich heritage is evident in its language, traditions, and remarkable historical sites. Join us in the as we explore the breathtaking natural landscapes and outdoor activities that Slovenia has to offer.

Chapter 7: Language and People of Slovenia

Introduction:

As you embark on your journey through Slovenia, it is essential to familiarize yourself with the language and customs of the local people. This chapter will provide you with a brief overview of the languages spoken in Slovenia, along with some common phrases to help you navigate your way through this beautiful country. Additionally, we will explore the social customs and etiquette that will ensure you have a memorable and respectful experience during your stay.

Languages Spoken in Slovenia:

Slovene, also known as Slovenian, is the official language of Slovenia. It belongs to the South Slavic group of languages and shares similarities with Croatian and Serbian. While Slovene is the predominant language spoken by the majority of Slovenians, many locals also have a good command of English, especially in tourist areas. You may also find that German and Italian are spoken in certain regions, particularly near the borders.

Common Phrases:

Learning a few basic phrases in the local language can go a long way in enhancing your travel experience and connecting with the Slovenian people. Here are some common phrases to get you started:

1. Hello - Zdravo (ZDRAH-voh)

2. Goodbye - Nasvidenje (NAHS-vee-DEN-yeh)

3. Please - Prosim (PROH-seem)

4. Thank you - Hvala (HVAH-lah)

5. Yes - Da (dah)

6. No - Ne (neh)

7. Excuse me - Oprostite (oh-PROHS-tee-teh)

8. Do you speak English? - Govorite angleško? (GOH-voh-ree-teh ahn-GLEHSH-koh?)

9. Where is...? - Kje je...? (kyeh yeh...?)

10. Cheers! - Na zdravje! (nah ZDRAH-vee-yeh)

Language Tips for Travelers:

While English is widely understood in Slovenia, it is always appreciated when visitors make an effort to communicate in the local language. Here are some language tips to help you navigate your way through Slovenia:

1. Carry a phrasebook or use language translation apps to assist you in basic communication.

2. Learn a few key phrases and greetings to show respect and make a positive impression.

3. Be patient and speak slowly when communicating with locals who may have limited English proficiency.

4. Use simple gestures or visual aids to overcome language barriers when necessary.

5. Always ask politely if someone speaks English before assuming they do.

6. Learn the basic rules of pronunciation in Slovene to make your attempts at speaking the language more effective.

Social Customs and Etiquette:

To fully immerse yourself in the Slovenian culture, understanding the social customs and etiquette is crucial. Here are some key points to keep in mind:

1. Greetings: When meeting someone for the first time, a handshake is the most common form of greeting. Maintain eye contact and use a friendly tone.

2. Punctuality: Slovenians value punctuality, so it is important to arrive on time for appointments and social gatherings.

3. Dining Etiquette: When invited to a Slovenian home, it is customary to bring a small gift for the host. Table manners are generally formal, with the European style of dining being followed.

4. Tipping: Tipping is customary in Slovenia, and it is customary to leave a 10% tip in restaurants, cafes, and bars unless a service charge is already included.

5. Dress Code: Slovenians tend to dress smartly and conservatively, especially in formal settings. It is advisable to dress neatly and avoid overly casual attire.

Conclusion:

Understanding the language and customs of Slovenia is a valuable tool for any traveler. By taking the time to learn a few basic phrases, respecting the local customs, and embracing the Slovenian way of life, you will undoubtedly create lasting memories and meaningful connections during your visit to this enchanting country.

Chapter 8: Traditional Cuisine of Slovenia

Introduction:

Slovenia, a hidden gem nestled in the heart of Europe, offers a culinary experience that is as diverse as its landscape. With influences from neighboring countries such as Italy, Austria, Hungary, and Croatia, Slovenian cuisine boasts a unique blend of flavors and traditional dishes that are sure to delight any food enthusiast. In this chapter, we will explore the rich and vibrant culinary heritage of Slovenia, from its most popular dishes and ingredients to where you can find the best food in the country. Additionally, we will provide you with cooking tips and recipes, allowing you to bring a taste of Slovenia into your own kitchen.

1. A Taste of Tradition:

Slovenian cuisine is deeply rooted in tradition, with recipes passed down through generations. The use of fresh, locally sourced ingredients is a cornerstone of this culinary heritage. From the rolling hills of the countryside to the coastal regions, each area of Slovenia has its own unique dishes and specialties.

2. Popular Dishes:

a) Potica: This traditional Slovenian pastry is a must-try. Made with a delicate yeast dough and filled with various sweet or savory fillings, such as walnuts, poppy seeds, or cottage cheese, potica is a true culinary masterpiece.

b) Kranjska Klobasa: Known as the Carniolan sausage, this Slovenian delicacy is made from high-quality pork and seasoned with garlic, salt, and pepper. It is often served with sauerkraut and mustard, making it a popular choice among locals and visitors alike.

c) Štruklji: These rolled dumplings are a comfort food staple in Slovenia. They can be filled with a variety of ingredients, such as cottage cheese, walnuts, or even tarragon. Served with a dollop of sour cream, štruklji are a true delight.

d) Idrijski Žlikrofi: Hailing from the town of Idrija, these small potato dumplings are a specialty of the region. They are typically filled with a mixture of herbs and served with melted butter and breadcrumbs.

3. Ingredients:

Slovenian cuisine celebrates the abundance of fresh, seasonal ingredients available throughout the year. From forest mushrooms and wild game to locally sourced honey and dairy products, the country's culinary scene is a testament to its rich agricultural heritage.

4. Where to Find the Best Food:

When it comes to experiencing the best of Slovenian cuisine, exploring the local markets and traditional restaurants is a must. Ljubljana, the capital city, offers a wide range of culinary delights, from trendy eateries to traditional taverns. Additionally, the coastal towns of Piran and Koper are known for their seafood specialties, while the Alpine region of Bled and Bohinj offers hearty mountain fare.

5. Cooking Tips and Recipes:

To truly immerse yourself in the flavors of Slovenia, we have included a few traditional recipes for you to try at home. From the famous potica to the comforting štruklji, these recipes will transport you to the heart of Slovenian cuisine.

Conclusion:

Slovenia's traditional cuisine is a reflection of its rich cultural heritage and diverse landscape. From the hearty mountain fare to the delicate pastries, there is something to satisfy every palate. By exploring the local markets, traditional restaurants, and trying your hand at Slovenian recipes, you will embark on a culinary journey that will leave you craving more. So, come and savor the flavors of Slovenia, a country where tradition and innovation meet on every plate.

Chapter 9: Modern Cuisine of Slovenia

Introduction:

Welcome to the culinary journey through Slovenia, a country that has recently emerged as a hidden gem in the world of gastronomy. In this chapter, we will explore the modern cuisine of Slovenia, its most popular dishes and ingredients, where to find the best food in the country, and even provide you with some cooking tips and recipes to try at home. Get ready to tantalize your taste buds and discover the unique flavors of Slovenia!

1. A Fusion of Tradition and Innovation:

Slovenian cuisine beautifully blends traditional recipes with modern techniques, resulting in a culinary experience that is both authentic and innovative. Chefs across the country have embraced the use of local, seasonal ingredients to create dishes that reflect the diverse landscape and cultural influences of Slovenia.

2. Traditional Dishes with a Modern Twist:

While traditional Slovenian dishes such as potica (rolled pastry with various fillings), štruklji (rolled dumplings), and kranjska klobasa (Carniolan sausage) still hold a special place in the hearts of locals, modern cuisine has introduced exciting variations to these classics. Imagine potica filled with unique combinations like pumpkin and goat cheese or štruklji stuffed with truffles and wild mushrooms. These innovative twists on traditional dishes are sure to surprise and delight your taste buds.

3. The Influence of Neighboring Countries:

Slovenia's geographical location has allowed it to absorb culinary influences from neighboring countries such as Italy, Austria, Hungary, and Croatia. These influences can be seen in dishes like štruklji, which resemble Italian cannelloni, and gibanica, a layered pastry similar to the Hungarian dobos torte. Exploring the modern cuisine of Slovenia means experiencing a harmonious blend of flavors from various European culinary traditions.

4. Popular Ingredients:

Slovenia's diverse landscape provides an abundance of fresh and high-quality ingredients. From the fertile plains of Prekmurje to the stunning Julian Alps, the country offers a rich array of produce, meats, and dairy products. Look out for ingredients like pumpkin seed oil, buckwheat, forest mushrooms, freshwater fish, and the famous Tolminc cheese. These ingredients form the backbone of many Slovenian dishes and contribute to their unique flavors.

5. Where to Find the Best Food:

To truly experience the modern cuisine of Slovenia, venture beyond the typical tourist spots and explore local restaurants and farm-to-table establishments. Ljubljana, the capital city, is a great starting point, with its vibrant food scene and a wide range of culinary offerings. Additionally, the coastal towns of Piran and Koper are known for their fresh seafood delicacies, while the countryside offers charming guesthouses and farm stays where you can savor traditional dishes prepared with love and care.

6. Cooking Tips and Recipes:

To bring a taste of Slovenia to your own kitchen, we have included some cooking tips and recipes that showcase the flavors of this beautiful country. From hearty stews to delicate pastries, these recipes are designed to be approachable yet authentic, allowing you to recreate the magic of Slovenian cuisine in your own home.

Conclusion:

The modern cuisine of Slovenia is a testament to the country's rich culinary heritage and its embrace of innovation. By blending tradition with modern techniques, Slovenian chefs have created a unique and exciting food culture that is sure to captivate your senses. Whether you're exploring local restaurants or trying your hand at cooking

Slovenian dishes at home, be prepared to embark on a gastronomic adventure like no other.

Chapter 10: Drinks and Beverages of Slovenia

Introduction:

Slovenia, a hidden gem in the heart of Europe, not only offers breathtaking landscapes and rich cultural heritage but also boasts a wide variety of delightful drinks and beverages. From traditional spirits to refreshing non-alcoholic beverages, Slovenia has something to satisfy every palate. In this chapter, we will explore the diverse world of Slovenian drinks and beverages, highlighting the most popular choices and where to find the best drinking experiences in the country.

1. Traditional Alcoholic Beverages:

1.1. Slovenian Wine: Slovenia is renowned for its exceptional wines, with vineyards scattered throughout the country. The wine regions of Podravje, Primorska, and Posavje produce a wide range of white, red, and sparkling wines. Don't miss the opportunity to taste the internationally acclaimed Rebula, Refošk, and Cviček varieties.

1.2. Rakija: A traditional fruit brandy, rakija holds a special place in Slovenian culture. Made from various fruits like plums, pears, or cherries, rakija is a strong spirit that warms the soul. Try it as an aperitif or a digestive, and savor the unique flavors that each region's rakija offers.

1.3. Craft Beers: In recent years, Slovenia has experienced a craft beer revolution. Microbreweries have been popping up all over the country, offering an array of flavors and styles. From hoppy IPAs to rich stouts, beer enthusiasts will find a diverse selection to explore.

2. Non-Alcoholic Beverages:

2.1. Mineral Water: Slovenia is blessed with an abundance of natural springs, resulting in high-quality mineral water. Locals and visitors alike enjoy the refreshing taste and health benefits of Slovenian mineral water. Look for brands like Radenska, Donat, or Rogaška while exploring the country.

2.2. Herbal Teas: Slovenia's pristine nature provides an ideal environment for growing aromatic herbs. Herbal teas made from locally sourced ingredients are popular throughout the country. Experience the soothing effects of chamomile, linden flower, or sage tea, which can be found in cafes, tearooms, and even traditional mountain huts.

2.3. Elderflower Syrup: A staple in Slovenian households, elderflower syrup is a sweet and floral non-alcoholic beverage. Diluted with water, it creates a refreshing and thirst-quenching drink, perfect for hot summer days. You can find this delightful syrup in local markets or try it in traditional Slovenian desserts.

3. Where to Find the Best Drinks in Slovenia:

3.1. Ljubljana: The capital city is a vibrant hub for culinary experiences, including a wide range of bars, pubs, and wine cellars. Explore the streets of Ljubljana's Old Town to discover hidden gems offering a variety of drinks to suit all tastes.

3.2. Maribor: Known as the wine capital of Slovenia, Maribor is a must-visit destination for wine enthusiasts. Visit the Old Vine House, home to the oldest vine in the world, and enjoy wine tastings in the nearby vineyards.

3.3. Coastal Towns: The coastal region of Slovenia, including Piran and Portorož, offers a unique blend of Mediterranean flavors. Indulge in local wines and seafood delicacies while enjoying the stunning views of the Adriatic Sea.

Conclusion:

Slovenia's drinks and beverages reflect the country's rich cultural heritage and natural abundance. Whether you prefer a glass of exquisite wine, a sip of traditional rakija, or a refreshing non-alcoholic beverage, Slovenia has it all. With its diverse offerings and unique drinking experiences, exploring the drinks and beverages of Slovenia is an essential part of any visit to this enchanting country.

Chapter 11: Dining out in Slovenia

Introduction:

Slovenia, a hidden gem in the heart of Europe, offers a delightful culinary experience that reflects its diverse culture and rich history. From traditional hearty dishes to modern gastronomic delights, the Slovenian cuisine is sure to tantalize your taste buds. In this chapter, we will guide you through the art of dining out in Slovenia, providing tips on choosing the perfect restaurant, ordering food, and settling the bill. Additionally, we will recommend some exceptional restaurants across different regions of the country, ensuring you savor the best of Slovenian cuisine.

Choosing the Perfect Restaurant:

1. Authenticity is Key: Seek out restaurants that showcase traditional Slovenian cuisine. Look for those that emphasize locally sourced ingredients and traditional cooking methods, as they are more likely to provide an authentic experience.

2. Local Recommendations: Ask locals or consult reputable travel guides for recommendations. Locals often know the best-hidden gems that may not be as well-known to tourists.

3. Ambiance and Setting: Consider the ambiance and setting that align with your preferences. Slovenia offers a range of dining options, from charming countryside taverns to elegant city restaurants. Choose a setting that complements your desired dining experience.

Ordering Food:

1. Slovenian Specialties: Embrace the opportunity to try traditional Slovenian dishes. Don't miss out on delights such as Potica (rolled pastry with various fillings), Kranjska klobasa (Carniolan sausage), and Štruklji (rolled dumplings). Be adventurous and explore the diverse regional cuisines Slovenia has to offer.

2. Seasonal Delicacies: Take advantage of seasonal ingredients. Slovenian cuisine is strongly influenced by the changing seasons, with

each offering its own unique flavors. Ask your server for recommendations based on the current season's specialties.

3. Wine Pairing: Slovenia is renowned for its exceptional wines. Pair your meal with a local wine, as Slovenian vineyards produce a wide variety of high-quality wines. Seek advice from your server or sommelier for the perfect wine pairing to enhance your dining experience.

Settling the Bill:

1. Tipping Etiquette: In Slovenia, tipping is not obligatory but is appreciated. It is customary to round up the bill or leave a 10% tip if you are satisfied with the service. However, tipping is entirely at your discretion.

2. Payment Methods: Most restaurants in Slovenia accept credit cards, but it is advisable to carry some cash, especially when dining in smaller establishments or rural areas. Ensure you have the local currency, the Euro, readily available.

Recommended Restaurants in Slovenia:

1. Ljubljana: Strelec Restaurant - Located in Ljubljana Castle, Strelec offers a unique dining experience with a stunning view of the city. Indulge in their modern interpretation of Slovenian cuisine, accompanied by an extensive wine list.

2. Bled: Vila Bled Restaurant - Situated in a historic villa on the shores of Lake Bled, this restaurant offers a refined dining experience. Enjoy their gourmet menu, featuring seasonal ingredients and impeccable service.

3. Piran: Rizi Bizi - Nestled in the charming coastal town of Piran, Rizi Bizi serves traditional Istrian dishes with a modern twist. Relish their seafood specialties while enjoying the picturesque views of the Adriatic Sea.

4. Maribor: Hiša Denk - Located in Slovenia's second-largest city, Hiša Denk is known for its innovative cuisine and exceptional wine

pairings. Experience their tasting menu, which beautifully combines local flavors with contemporary techniques.

Conclusion:

Dining out in Slovenia is not just about satisfying your hunger; it is a journey through the country's rich culinary heritage. By following our tips on choosing the perfect restaurant, ordering food, and settling the bill, you can fully immerse yourself in the Slovenian dining experience. Remember to explore the recommended restaurants across Slovenia, as they offer a true taste of the country's diverse and delicious cuisine.

Chapter 12: Food and Drink Festivals in Slovenia

Introduction:

Slovenia, a hidden gem nestled in the heart of Europe, is not only known for its breathtaking landscapes and rich cultural heritage but also for its vibrant food and drink festivals. Slovenians take immense pride in their culinary traditions, and these festivals offer a unique opportunity for locals and tourists alike to indulge in a gastronomic adventure. In this chapter, we will explore some of the major food and drink festivals that take place throughout the year in Slovenia.

1. Gourmet Ljubljana:

Kicking off the festival calendar is Gourmet Ljubljana, a celebration of the capital city's diverse culinary scene. Held in early spring, this festival brings together top chefs, local producers, and food enthusiasts to showcase the best of Slovenian cuisine. Visitors can sample a wide array of dishes, from traditional delicacies to modern interpretations, while enjoying live music and entertainment in the heart of Ljubljana.

2. Maribor Wine Festival:

As the oldest wine festival in Slovenia, the Maribor Wine Festival is a must-visit for wine enthusiasts. Taking place in the charming city of Maribor, this event celebrates the rich wine-making heritage of the region. Visitors can taste an extensive selection of local wines, attend educational workshops, and experience the vibrant atmosphere of the festival. The highlight of the event is the traditional Old Vine procession, where participants parade through the streets carrying the world's oldest vine.

3. Piran Salt Pans Festival:

For those with a taste for the salty side of life, the Piran Salt Pans Festival is an unforgettable experience. Located on the picturesque

Slovenian coast, this festival pays homage to the centuries-old tradition of salt production. Visitors can witness the harvesting process firsthand, learn about the history and significance of salt, and of course, savor the unique flavors of salt-inspired dishes prepared by renowned chefs. The festival also features cultural performances and exhibitions, adding an extra layer of enchantment to the event.

4. Ptuj Carnival:

While not strictly a food and drink festival, the Ptuj Carnival deserves a mention for its culinary significance. This centuries-old tradition, recognized as one of the most authentic carnivals in Europe, showcases the vibrant spirit of Slovenian folklore. During the carnival, the streets of Ptuj come alive with colorful parades, traditional costumes, and lively music. Local delicacies, such as krofi (traditional doughnuts) and kurentovanje sausage, are abundantly available, allowing visitors to immerse themselves in the festive atmosphere while savoring the flavors of Slovenian cuisine.

5. Chocolate Festival Radovljica:

Indulge your sweet tooth at the Chocolate Festival Radovljica, a paradise for chocolate lovers. Held in the charming town of Radovljica, this festival celebrates all things chocolate. Visitors can explore a variety of chocolate-themed exhibitions, participate in workshops, and, of course, taste an array of delectable chocolate creations. From truffles to pralines, this festival is a haven for those with a passion for the cocoa bean.

Conclusion:

Slovenia's food and drink festivals offer a delightful blend of culinary traditions, cultural experiences, and vibrant atmospheres. Whether you're a wine connoisseur, a lover of traditional cuisine, or simply seeking a unique gastronomic adventure, these festivals provide an excellent opportunity to indulge in Slovenia's rich culinary heritage. Plan your visit accordingly, and be prepared to savor the flavors and immerse yourself in the festive spirit of these extraordinary events.

Chapter 13: Getting to Slovenia

Introduction:

Slovenia, a hidden gem nestled in the heart of Europe, offers breathtaking landscapes, rich cultural heritage, and warm hospitality. To embark on your Slovenian adventure, it is essential to know the various modes of transportation available to reach this enchanting country. In this chapter, we will explore the different ways to get to Slovenia, including by plane, train, bus, car, and ferry. Whether you prefer convenience, affordability, or scenic routes, Slovenia welcomes you with open arms.

1. By Plane:

Slovenia boasts an efficient network of international airports, making air travel a popular choice for visitors. The main airport, Jože Pučnik Airport, located near the capital city of Ljubljana, offers direct flights from major European cities and international hubs. With several airlines operating regular routes, you can easily find a suitable flight to Slovenia. Upon arrival, you can conveniently rent a car or use public transportation to explore the country.

2. By Train:

For those seeking a scenic journey, traveling to Slovenia by train is an excellent option. The country is well-connected to neighboring countries, including Austria, Italy, Hungary, and Croatia, through an extensive rail network. The trains are comfortable, reliable, and offer breathtaking views of Slovenia's picturesque landscapes. Arriving at the main train stations in Ljubljana or Maribor, you can easily access other parts of the country using local trains, buses, or taxis.

3. By Bus:

Traveling to Slovenia by bus is a cost-effective and convenient choice, especially for those exploring nearby European countries. Numerous international bus companies operate regular routes to major Slovenian cities, providing a budget-friendly alternative to other modes of transportation. The central bus stations in Ljubljana and Maribor serve as major hubs, offering connections to various destinations within Slovenia.

4. By Car:

If you prefer the freedom and flexibility of driving, reaching Slovenia by car allows you to explore the country at your own pace. Slovenia has an excellent road infrastructure, with well-maintained highways and scenic routes. Bordering countries, such as Austria, Italy, Hungary, and Croatia, offer easy access to Slovenia by road. It is important to note that a vignette, a toll sticker, is required to use Slovenian highways. These can be purchased at border crossings, gas stations, or online.

5. By Ferry:

For those seeking a unique and leisurely journey, arriving in Slovenia by ferry is an option worth considering. Slovenia has a small coastline along the Adriatic Sea, and the Port of Koper serves as the main gateway for ferry arrivals. Regular ferry services connect Koper to various Italian ports, such as Venice and Trieste, providing a scenic and relaxing way to enter Slovenia.

Conclusion:

No matter which mode of transportation you choose, reaching Slovenia is an accessible and enjoyable experience. Whether you opt for the convenience of air travel, the scenic routes of train or bus, the freedom of driving, or the leisurely ferry ride, Slovenia awaits with its natural beauty, cultural treasures, and warm hospitality. Plan your journey wisely, considering your preferences and priorities, and get ready to embark on a memorable adventure in Slovenia, a truly captivating destination in the heart of Europe.

Chapter 14: Exploring Slovenia's Public Transportation Network

Introduction:

Welcome to Slovenia, a country known for its breathtaking landscapes, charming towns, and rich cultural heritage. To truly immerse yourself in the beauty of this hidden gem, it's essential to understand the various modes of public transportation available. In this chapter, we will explore the different types of public transportation in Slovenia, including trains, buses, and metros, and provide you with a comprehensive guide to navigating the capital city's transportation system.

1. Trains: Efficient and Scenic Journeys

Slovenia's train network is renowned for its efficiency and scenic routes. Whether you're traveling from Ljubljana, the capital, to the picturesque Lake Bled or venturing into the Julian Alps, trains offer a comfortable and convenient mode of transportation. With well-connected routes and frequent departures, you can easily explore Slovenia's diverse regions while enjoying the stunning landscapes passing by your window.

2. Buses: Connecting Every Corner

When it comes to exploring the nooks and crannies of Slovenia, buses are your best friend. The country boasts an extensive bus network that connects even the most remote areas. From charming coastal towns like Piran to the enchanting vineyards of the Vipava Valley, buses offer a reliable and affordable means of transportation. Additionally, Slovenia's eco-friendly approach ensures that buses are equipped with modern amenities and adhere to strict environmental standards.

3. Metros: Navigating Ljubljana's Capital

Ljubljana, Slovenia's vibrant capital, is well-served by its efficient metro system. Although not as extensive as other European capitals,

Ljubljana's metro network covers the city's main areas, making it easy for tourists to get around. With regular schedules and -friendly ticketing systems, exploring Ljubljana's attractions, such as the iconic Triple Bridge or the Ljubljana Castle, becomes a hassle-free experience.

4. The Capital City's Public Transportation Map

To assist you in navigating Ljubljana's public transportation system, we have included a comprehensive map in this chapter. This map highlights the metro lines, bus routes, and train stations, enabling you to plan your journeys effectively. Additionally, the map also indicates major landmarks, popular tourist attractions, and essential amenities, ensuring that you can easily find your way around the city.

Conclusion:

Slovenia's public transportation system offers a convenient and efficient way to explore this captivating country. From the scenic train routes that traverse the breathtaking landscapes to the extensive bus network that connects every corner, getting around Slovenia has never been easier. In Ljubljana, the metro system provides a seamless way to discover the city's hidden treasures. With this chapter as your guide, you are well-equipped to embark on an unforgettable adventure through Slovenia's public transportation network.

Chapter 15: Types of Accommodation in Slovenia

Introduction:

When planning a trip to Slovenia, one of the key aspects to consider is the type of accommodation that suits your preferences and budget. Slovenia offers a diverse range of accommodations, ranging from luxurious hotels to cozy guesthouses and budget-friendly hostels. Additionally, with the rise of alternative accommodation options like Airbnbs, travelers now have even more choices. In this chapter, we will explore the various types of accommodation available in Slovenia, providing you with valuable insights to help you make an informed decision.

1. Hotels:

Slovenia boasts a wide array of hotels, catering to different budgets and preferences. From luxurious five-star establishments in major cities like Ljubljana and Maribor to charming boutique hotels nestled in picturesque towns, there is something to suit every traveler's taste. Whether you seek modern amenities, spa facilities, or breathtaking views, hotels in Slovenia offer a comfortable and convenient stay.

2. Hostels:

Ideal for budget-conscious travelers or those seeking a more social atmosphere, hostels in Slovenia provide affordable accommodations with shared facilities such as kitchens and common areas. They are particularly popular among backpackers and solo travelers, offering a chance to meet like-minded adventurers. Hostels can be found in major cities like Bled, Ljubljana, and Piran, as well as in smaller towns, providing a cost-effective option for exploring Slovenia.

3. Guesthouses:

For a more personal and authentic experience, consider staying in a guesthouse. These family-run establishments offer cozy rooms and often include breakfast made from locally sourced ingredients. Guesthouses can be found throughout Slovenia, especially in rural areas, where you can immerse yourself in the local culture, savor traditional cuisine, and receive personalized recommendations from your hosts.

4. Airbnbs:

With the rise of the sharing economy, Airbnb has become a popular choice for travelers seeking unique and affordable accommodations in Slovenia. From apartments in the heart of Ljubljana to countryside cottages surrounded by nature, Airbnb offers a wide range of options to suit different preferences and group sizes. Staying in an Airbnb allows you to experience Slovenia like a local, providing a more intimate and immersive travel experience.

5. Farm Stays:

For those seeking a tranquil escape and a taste of Slovenia's rural life, farm stays are an excellent option. These accommodations allow you to stay on working farms, where you can participate in daily activities, such as milking cows or harvesting crops. Farm stays provide a unique opportunity to connect with nature, enjoy homemade meals prepared with farm-fresh ingredients, and experience the peaceful countryside.

Conclusion:

Choosing the right accommodation is crucial for a memorable trip to Slovenia. Whether you prefer the comfort of hotels, the social atmosphere of hostels, the personalized experience of guesthouses, the local touch of Airbnbs, or the tranquility of farm stays, Slovenia offers a variety of options to cater to every traveler's needs. Consider your budget, preferences, and desired experience when selecting your accommodation, and enjoy your stay in this beautiful country.

Chapter 16: Tips for Staying in Slovenia

Welcome to Slovenia! This charming country nestled in the heart of Europe offers a wealth of natural beauty, cultural heritage, and warm hospitality. As you embark on your Slovenian adventure, here are some invaluable tips to ensure a smooth and memorable stay.

1. Booking Accommodation:

a) Research and book in advance: Slovenia is becoming an increasingly popular tourist destination, especially during peak seasons. To secure the best accommodation options, it is advisable to book well in advance.

b) Consider diverse options: From luxurious hotels to cozy guesthouses and budget-friendly hostels, Slovenia offers a wide range of accommodation choices. Explore different options based on your preferences and budget.

c) Stay in local neighborhoods: To experience the authentic Slovenian way of life, consider staying in local neighborhoods rather than solely focusing on tourist areas. This will allow you to immerse yourself in the local culture and discover hidden gems.

2. Getting Around:

a) Public transportation: Slovenia boasts an efficient and well-connected public transportation system. Utilize trains, buses, and trams to navigate between cities and towns. Consider purchasing a Slovenia Tourist Card, which offers unlimited travel on public transport and various discounts.

b) Rent a car: If you prefer flexibility and independence, renting a car is an excellent option. Slovenia's road network is well-maintained, and driving allows you to explore the country's picturesque landscapes at your own pace.

c) Cycling and hiking: For nature enthusiasts, Slovenia offers an extensive network of cycling and hiking trails. Rent a bicycle or lace up your hiking boots to explore the breathtaking scenery, picturesque villages, and charming vineyards.

3. Staying Safe:

a) Emergency numbers: Familiarize yourself with Slovenia's emergency numbers, including 112 for general emergencies, 113 for police, and 112 for medical assistance. Keep these numbers handy in case of any unforeseen circumstances.

b) Respect local laws and customs: Slovenia is known for its friendly and law-abiding society. To ensure a safe and pleasant stay, respect local laws, customs, and traditions. Familiarize yourself with Slovenian etiquette, such as greeting locals with a handshake and removing your shoes when entering someone's home.

c) Take necessary precautions: While Slovenia is generally a safe country, it is always wise to take basic precautions. Keep your valuables secure, be aware of your surroundings, and avoid isolated areas, especially at night.

4. Cultural Etiquette:

a) Language: Slovenian is the official language of Slovenia. Although many locals speak English, learning a few basic Slovenian phrases will be greatly appreciated by the locals.

b) Tipping: Tipping is not obligatory in Slovenia, as a service charge is usually included in the bill. However, it is customary to leave a small tip if you receive exceptional service.

c) Dress code: Slovenians generally dress conservatively, especially when visiting religious sites or dining at upscale restaurants. It is advisable to dress modestly and avoid wearing revealing clothing in such settings.

By following these tips, you are sure to have an unforgettable experience while staying in Slovenia. Embrace the country's natural wonders, immerse yourself in its rich culture, and savor the warm hospitality of the Slovenian people. Enjoy your journey through this hidden gem of Europe!

Chapter 17: Must-See Attractions in Slovenia

Introduction:

Slovenia, a hidden gem in the heart of Europe, offers a myriad of breathtaking attractions that will leave any traveler in awe. From picturesque landscapes to charming cities, this chapter will guide you through the top 10 must-see attractions in Slovenia. Prepare to be captivated by the country's natural beauty, rich history, and warm hospitality.

1. Lake Bled:

Nestled amidst the Julian Alps, Lake Bled is a fairytale-like destination that will steal your heart. The emerald-green lake is adorned with a tiny island housing the iconic Bled Castle, which offers panoramic views of the surrounding mountains. Don't miss the opportunity to take a traditional Pletna boat ride to the island and ring the church bell for good luck.

2. Ljubljana:

The capital city of Slovenia, Ljubljana, is a vibrant and charming place that effortlessly blends history with modernity. Stroll along the Ljubljanica River, cross the iconic Triple Bridge, and explore the medieval Ljubljana Castle perched atop a hill. Discover the city's lively café culture, picturesque streets, and vibrant markets, making Ljubljana a must-visit destination.

3. Postojna Cave:

Embark on an underground adventure at the Postojna Cave, one of the largest and most captivating cave systems in Europe. Hop aboard the electric train and journey through a mesmerizing labyrinth of stalactites, stalagmites, and limestone formations. Marvel at the unique beauty of the Concert Hall, the Brilliant Passage, and the Spaghetti Hall, leaving you in awe of nature's wonders.

4. Triglav National Park:

For nature enthusiasts, Triglav National Park is a must-see attraction. Located in the Julian Alps, it is Slovenia's only national park, offering a pristine alpine environment. Hike through breathtaking valleys, crystal-clear lakes, and majestic mountains. Don't miss the opportunity to conquer Mount Triglav, the country's highest peak, for an unforgettable adventure.

5. Piran:

Nestled on the Adriatic coastline, the charming town of Piran will transport you to a bygone era. Wander through narrow cobblestone streets, admire the Venetian Gothic architecture, and soak up the Mediterranean atmosphere. Climb the bell tower of the St. George's Parish Church for panoramic views of the town and the shimmering sea.

6. Škocjan Caves:

Listed as a UNESCO World Heritage site, the Škocjan Caves are a natural wonder that will leave you speechless. Embark on a guided tour through the underground labyrinth, crossing breathtaking bridges and witnessing the power of the Reka River, which carved out this magnificent cave system over millions of years.

7. Lake Bohinj:

Escape to the tranquility of Lake Bohinj, Slovenia's largest permanent lake, nestled in the heart of the Julian Alps. Surrounded by pristine forests and towering mountains, this natural paradise offers a wide range of activities, including hiking, biking, and swimming. Take a cable car to Mount Vogel for stunning panoramic views of the lake and the Triglav National Park.

8. Predjama Castle:

Perched dramatically in the mouth of a cave, Predjama Castle is a medieval marvel that will ignite your imagination. Explore the secret passages, hidden chambers, and grand halls of this architectural gem, which has stood for over 800 years. Learn about the legendary knight Erazem, whose daring escapes from the castle made him a local hero.

9. Maribor:

Discover the vibrant city of Maribor, located in the heart of Slovenia's wine region. Explore the charming old town, visit the Maribor Castle, and wander through the lively Lent district along the Drava River. Don't miss the opportunity to taste the world-renowned wines of the Maribor Wine Road, which winds through picturesque vineyards.

10. Vintgar Gorge:

Immerse yourself in the natural beauty of the Vintgar Gorge, a true paradise for nature lovers. Follow the wooden walkways and bridges that meander along the Radovna River, leading you through narrow canyons and past stunning waterfalls. The emerald-green water and lush vegetation create a magical atmosphere that will leave you breathless.

Conclusion:

Slovenia's must-see attractions offer a diverse range of experiences, from enchanting lakes and caves to charming cities and alpine landscapes. Whether you seek adventure, relaxation, or cultural immersion, this chapter has provided you with a glimpse of the wonders that await in this captivating country. Embark on your Slovenian adventure and create memories that will last a lifetime.

Chapter 18: Natural Wonders of Slovenia

Introduction:

Slovenia, a small but enchanting country nestled in the heart of Europe, is blessed with an abundance of natural wonders. From majestic mountains to crystal-clear lakes and pristine forests, this hidden gem offers a diverse range of landscapes that will leave any nature enthusiast in awe. In this chapter, we will explore the top 10 natural wonders of Slovenia, each offering a unique and breathtaking experience.

1. Triglav National Park:

Nestled in the Julian Alps, Triglav National Park is a haven for outdoor enthusiasts. Home to Slovenia's highest peak, Mount Triglav, this park boasts dramatic mountain ranges, glacial valleys, and picturesque alpine meadows. Visitors can embark on thrilling hikes, climb challenging rock faces, or simply immerse themselves in the tranquil beauty of this pristine wilderness.

2. Lake Bled:

No visit to Slovenia is complete without a trip to Lake Bled, a true natural masterpiece. With its emerald-green waters, a tiny island crowned by a church, and a medieval castle perched on a cliff, this enchanting lake is straight out of a fairy tale. Visitors can take a traditional wooden boat called a pletna to the island, ring the bell for good luck, and savor the breathtaking views from the castle.

3. Postojna Cave:

Venture underground to discover the mesmerizing Postojna Cave, one of the world's largest and most captivating karst caves. Embark on a guided tour through a labyrinth of stalactites, stalagmites, and underground chambers, and witness the stunning formations that have been sculpted over millions of years. Don't miss the unique experience of riding an underground train through this subterranean wonderland.

4. Lake Bohinj:

Tucked away in the Triglav National Park, Lake Bohinj is a tranquil retreat for those seeking solace in nature. Surrounded by towering mountains and dense forests, this glacial lake offers pristine waters perfect for swimming, kayaking, or simply relaxing on its peaceful shores. Hiking trails around the lake lead to hidden waterfalls and breathtaking viewpoints, providing endless opportunities for exploration.

5. Škocjan Caves:

Listed as a UNESCO World Heritage site, the Škocjan Caves are a testament to the extraordinary power of water. Explore the vast underground chambers, witness the roaring Reka River as it disappears into the abyss, and marvel at the awe-inspiring stalactites and stalagmites that adorn this subterranean wonderland. The sheer magnitude of these caves will leave you speechless.

6. Soča River:

Renowned for its crystal-clear turquoise waters, the Soča River is a paradise for adventure seekers. Flowing through the Julian Alps, this emerald gem offers thrilling opportunities for whitewater rafting, kayaking, and canyoning. As you navigate the rapids and marvel at the surrounding alpine scenery, you'll understand why the Soča River is often referred to as the Emerald Beauty.

7. Logar Valley:

Nestled in the Kamnik-Savinja Alps, the Logar Valley is a pristine alpine valley that exudes tranquility and natural beauty. Surrounded by majestic peaks, cascading waterfalls, and lush meadows, this hidden gem offers countless hiking trails for all levels of adventurers. Immerse yourself in the serenity of this valley, breathe in the fresh mountain air, and let its untouched charm captivate your soul.

8. Velika Planina:

Escape the hustle and bustle of modern life and step into a world frozen in time at Velika Planina. This high mountain plateau, dotted with traditional wooden huts, offers a glimpse into Slovenia's rich cultural heritage. Hike through the rolling meadows, interact with the shepherds tending their flocks, and savor the traditional dairy products that are still produced using age-old methods.

9. Lake Cerknica:

Prepare to witness a natural wonder that defies expectations. Lake Cerknica is a unique intermittent lake that magically appears and disappears throughout the year. Depending on the season and rainfall, the lake can transform from a vast expanse of water to a meandering river or even a lush meadow. Explore this ever-changing landscape and witness nature's captivating dance.

10. Vintgar Gorge:

Conclude your journey through Slovenia's natural wonders with a visit to Vintgar Gorge, a true paradise for nature lovers. Immerse yourself in the fairytale-like atmosphere as you walk along wooden bridges and pathways, passing emerald-green pools, cascading waterfalls, and towering cliffs. The sheer beauty and tranquility of this gorge make it a must-visit destination for any traveler.

Conclusion:

Slovenia's natural wonders are a testament to the country's remarkable diversity and pristine landscapes. From the towering peaks of the Julian Alps to the enchanting lakes, caves, and rivers, each destination offers a unique and awe-inspiring experience. Whether you're seeking adventure or simply yearning for tranquility, Slovenia's natural wonders are bound to leave an indelible mark on your heart and soul.

Chapter 19: Historical and Cultural Sites in Slovenia

Introduction:

Slovenia, a picturesque country nestled in the heart of Europe, is renowned for its rich historical and cultural heritage. From ancient castles to charming old towns, Slovenia offers a plethora of fascinating sites that take visitors on a journey through time. In this chapter, we will explore the top 10 historical and cultural sites in Slovenia, each offering a unique glimpse into the country's captivating past.

1. Ljubljana Castle, Ljubljana:

Perched atop a hill overlooking the capital city of Ljubljana, the Ljubljana Castle stands as a symbol of the city's resilience throughout history. Visitors can explore the castle's towers, ramparts, and exhibitions, delving into the city's medieval roots and the castle's significance as a strategic stronghold.

2. Lake Bled, Bled:

Nestled amidst the Julian Alps, Lake Bled is not only a natural wonder but also home to Bled Castle, perched on a cliff overlooking the lake. This medieval fortress offers breathtaking views and houses a museum that showcases the region's history, traditions, and legends.

3. Škocjan Caves, Divača:

A UNESCO World Heritage site, the Škocjan Caves are a mesmerizing underground wonderland. Visitors can explore the vast caverns, underground rivers, and awe-inspiring stalactite formations, gaining insight into the geological and cultural significance of this unique site.

4. Ptuj Castle, Ptuj:

Situated in the oldest town in Slovenia, Ptuj Castle is a captivating blend of architectural styles spanning centuries. This medieval fortress houses a museum that exhibits the town's history, art, and archaeological artifacts, providing visitors with a glimpse into Ptuj's rich past.

5. Predjama Castle, Postojna:

Nestled within a towering cliff, Predjama Castle is a true architectural marvel. Dating back to the 13th century, this enchanting castle offers a fascinating glimpse into medieval life, complete with secret tunnels and legends of daring knights.

6. Piran, Slovenian Coast:

The charming coastal town of Piran is a treasure trove of historical and cultural delights. Its well-preserved medieval architecture, narrow streets, and vibrant squares transport visitors back in time. The Tartini Square and St. George's Church are must-visit highlights.

7. Maribor Old Town, Maribor:

Maribor's Old Town exudes charm with its cobblestone streets, colorful facades, and medieval architecture. The town's iconic Lent district, home to the oldest vine in the world, invites visitors to explore its museums, galleries, and lively waterfront.

8. Postojna Cave, Postojna:

A true natural wonder, the Postojna Cave is the most visited cave in Europe. Visitors can embark on a captivating underground journey, marveling at the stunning limestone formations and encountering the unique olm, an endemic cave-dwelling amphibian.

9. Velika Planina, Kamnik:

Located in the Kamnik Alps, Velika Planina is a mountain plateau dotted with traditional wooden huts. This idyllic setting offers a glimpse into the traditional alpine life of Slovenian shepherds, providing visitors with an immersive cultural experience.

10. Ptuj, Ptuj:

The town of Ptuj, with its well-preserved medieval core, is a true gem for history enthusiasts. Visitors can explore its ancient streets, visit the Roman-era Ptuj Castle, and immerse themselves in the town's vibrant festivals and cultural traditions.

Conclusion:

Slovenia's historical and cultural sites offer a fascinating journey into the country's past. From medieval castles to underground caves, each site tells a unique story that reflects Slovenia's diverse heritage. Whether exploring the vibrant capital city or venturing into the picturesque countryside, visitors are sure to be captivated by the historical and cultural treasures that Slovenia has to offer.

Chapter 20: Museums and Art Galleries in Slovenia

Introduction:

Slovenia, a small but culturally rich country nestled in the heart of Europe, boasts a vibrant art scene and a plethora of museums that cater to every taste. From ancient artifacts to contemporary masterpieces, Slovenia's museums and art galleries offer a fascinating journey through the country's history, culture, and artistic expression. In this chapter, we will explore the top 10 museums and art galleries that should not be missed during your visit to Slovenia.

1. National Gallery of Slovenia, Ljubljana:

Located in the capital city, the National Gallery of Slovenia houses an extensive collection of Slovenian art spanning from the Middle Ages to the present day. From religious icons to modern installations, this gallery provides a comprehensive overview of Slovenian artistic heritage.

2. Museum of Modern Art (Moderna galerija), Ljubljana:

For those seeking contemporary art, the Museum of Modern Art in Ljubljana is a must-visit. With a focus on Slovenian and international modern and contemporary art, this museum showcases thought-provoking exhibitions that challenge traditional artistic boundaries.

3. Maribor Art Gallery, Maribor:

Situated in Slovenia's second-largest city, the Maribor Art Gallery is dedicated to promoting Slovenian and international contemporary art. With its diverse collection and rotating exhibitions, this gallery offers a unique perspective on the ever-evolving art scene.

4. Slovene Ethnographic Museum, Ljubljana:

Delve into Slovenia's rich cultural heritage at the Slovene Ethnographic Museum. This museum houses an extensive collection of ethnographic artifacts, showcasing the traditional customs, crafts, and lifestyles of various Slovenian regions.

5. Ptuj Castle, Ptuj:

Nestled in the picturesque town of Ptuj, Ptuj Castle is home to the Ptuj Regional Museum. Explore the castle's halls and chambers filled with historical artifacts, including archaeological finds, medieval weaponry, and artworks, providing insight into the region's history.

6. National Museum of Slovenia, Ljubljana:

Discover Slovenia's archaeological treasures and historical artifacts at the National Museum of Slovenia. From prehistoric times to the Roman period and beyond, this museum offers a comprehensive understanding of Slovenia's past.

7. Technical Museum of Slovenia, Bistra:

Located in the beautiful Bistra Castle near Ljubljana, the Technical Museum of Slovenia showcases the country's industrial and technological advancements. From vintage cars and steam engines to interactive displays, this museum offers an engaging experience for visitors of all ages.

8. Museum of Architecture and Design, Ljubljana:

Design enthusiasts will find inspiration at the Museum of Architecture and Design in Ljubljana. This museum exhibits contemporary architecture, industrial design, and visual communication, providing a platform for Slovenian designers to showcase their innovative works.

9. Ivan Grohar Gallery, Škofja Loka:

Step into the world of Slovenian painter Ivan Grohar at his eponymous gallery in Škofja Loka. This intimate museum displays the artist's stunning landscapes and portraits, allowing visitors to appreciate his contribution to Slovenian art.

10. Museum of Puppetry, Ljubljana:

For a whimsical experience, visit the Museum of Puppetry in Ljubljana. Explore the history of puppetry through an extensive collection of puppets, masks, and stage sets, and witness captivating puppet performances that bring these characters to life.

Conclusion:

Slovenia's museums and art galleries offer a diverse and enriching experience for art enthusiasts and history buffs alike. From ancient artifacts to contemporary creations, these cultural institutions provide a glimpse into Slovenia's rich heritage and artistic expression. With the top 10 museums and art galleries listed in this chapter, you are sure to embark on a captivating journey through Slovenia's vibrant art scene.

Chapter 21: Religious Sites in Slovenia

Introduction:

Slovenia, a small but culturally rich country nestled in the heart of Europe, boasts a diverse religious landscape that reflects its long and storied history. From ancient churches to tranquil monasteries, this chapter will take you on a spiritual journey through Slovenia's top ten religious sites. Immerse yourself in the country's religious heritage as you explore these unique destinations.

1. Ljubljana Cathedral (St. Nicholas's Church):

Located in the heart of Slovenia's capital city, Ljubljana Cathedral, also known as St. Nicholas's Church, stands as a magnificent example of Baroque architecture. Step inside to admire its ornate interior, adorned with stunning frescoes and intricate altars, and feel the serenity of this sacred space.

2. Bled Island Church:

Situated on a small island in the middle of Lake Bled, the Bled Island Church is a picturesque sight to behold. Accessible only by traditional wooden boats called pletnas, this charming church is a popular pilgrimage site. Climb the 99 stone steps to reach the church and ring the legendary wishing bell for good luck.

3. Maribor Cathedral (St. John the Baptist's Church):

Maribor Cathedral, dedicated to St. John the Baptist, is the largest church in Slovenia. Its Gothic architecture and stunning stained glass windows create an awe-inspiring atmosphere. Be sure to visit the nearby Plague Memorial, a poignant reminder of the city's history.

4. Ptuj Castle's Chapel of St. George:

Nestled within the walls of Ptuj Castle, the Chapel of St. George is a hidden gem. This Romanesque chapel, adorned with medieval frescoes, offers a glimpse into Slovenia's past. Marvel at the intricate artwork and soak in the tranquility of this sacred space.

5. Holy Trinity Church in Hrastovlje:

Located in the picturesque village of Hrastovlje, the Holy Trinity Church is renowned for its unique and well-preserved frescoes. Step inside this medieval church and be captivated by the vivid depictions of biblical scenes, including the famous Dance of Death.

6. Škocjan Caves and the Church of St. Cantius:

Explore the natural wonder of the Škocjan Caves, a UNESCO World Heritage Site, and discover the hidden Church of St. Cantius. Carved into the cave walls, this ancient church adds a spiritual element to the already awe-inspiring underground landscape.

7. Koper Cathedral (Assumption of Mary's Church):

Situated in the coastal town of Koper, the Assumption of Mary's Church is a stunning example of Venetian Gothic architecture. Admire the intricate details of its façade and step inside to marvel at the magnificent altarpiece created by the renowned artist Vittore Carpaccio.

8. Novo Mesto Cathedral (St. Nicholas's Church):

Novo Mesto Cathedral, dedicated to St. Nicholas, is a true architectural gem. Its blend of Gothic and Renaissance styles makes it a unique sight to behold. Explore the interior to admire its impressive vaulted ceilings and the exquisite works of art that adorn its walls.

9. Trsat Castle and Our Lady of Trsat Church:

Perched atop a hill overlooking the city of Rijeka, just across the Slovenian border, Trsat Castle is home to the Our Lady of Trsat Church. This Marian sanctuary attracts pilgrims from near and far, who come to pay their respects to the miraculous statue of the Virgin Mary.

10. Stična Abbey:

Conclude your spiritual journey at Stična Abbey, the oldest Cistercian monastery in Slovenia. Immerse yourself in the peaceful ambiance of this monastic complex, visit the abbey church, and explore the museum to learn about the rich history of the Cistercian order in Slovenia.

Conclusion:

Slovenia's religious sites offer a glimpse into the country's diverse spiritual heritage. Whether you seek architectural marvels, serene monastic retreats, or ancient frescoes, these top ten religious sites will not disappoint. Immerse yourself in Slovenia's rich history and spirituality as you explore these unique destinations.

Chapter 22: Outdoor Activities in Slovenia

Slovenia, a hidden gem nestled in the heart of Europe, offers a plethora of outdoor activities that will leave every adventure seeker in awe. From its majestic mountains to its crystal-clear lakes and charming coastal towns, this diverse country has something to offer for everyone. In this chapter, we will explore the top 10 outdoor activities in Slovenia that will undoubtedly ignite your sense of adventure and leave you with unforgettable memories.

1. Hiking in Triglav National Park:

Triglav National Park, named after Slovenia's highest peak, is a hiker's paradise. With over 800 kilometers of marked trails, you can explore breathtaking alpine landscapes, pristine lakes, and picturesque valleys. Don't miss the opportunity to conquer Mount Triglav itself, a challenging yet rewarding endeavor that offers panoramic views of the Julian Alps.

2. White Water Rafting on the Soča River:

For adrenaline junkies, white water rafting on the emerald green Soča River is an absolute must. Feel the rush as you navigate through thrilling rapids, surrounded by stunning canyons and unspoiled nature. This activity is suitable for both beginners and experienced rafters, making it a thrilling adventure for all.

3. Cycling along the Parenzana Trail:

Discover the Istrian Peninsula by cycling along the Parenzana Trail, a former railway line turned into a scenic cycling route. Pedal through charming villages, vineyards, and olive groves, enjoying breathtaking views of the Adriatic Sea. This leisurely activity allows you to immerse yourself in the region's rich history and indulge in delicious local cuisine along the way.

4. Paragliding in the Julian Alps:

Soar through the sky like a bird and experience Slovenia's mesmerizing landscapes from a different perspective. Paragliding in the Julian Alps offers a unique adventure, allowing you to witness the snow-capped peaks, lush valleys, and glistening lakes from above. Whether you're a seasoned paraglider or a first-timer, this thrilling activity will leave you in awe of Slovenia's natural beauty.

5. Canyoning in the Tolmin Gorges:

Embark on an exhilarating canyoning adventure in the Tolmin Gorges, a hidden gem in the Soča Valley. Descend through narrow gorges, jump into crystal-clear pools, and rappel down waterfalls, surrounded by breathtaking rock formations. This adrenaline-pumping activity will challenge your limits and provide an unforgettable experience in the heart of nature.

6. Stand-Up Paddleboarding on Lake Bled:

Experience tranquility and serenity as you glide across the iconic Lake Bled on a stand-up paddleboard. Marvel at the picturesque Bled Island and the medieval Bled Castle perched on a cliff while enjoying the calmness of the lake's crystal-clear waters. This activity is perfect for those seeking a peaceful and scenic adventure.

7. Skiing in Kranjska Gora:

During the winter months, Slovenia transforms into a winter wonderland, offering excellent skiing opportunities. Kranjska Gora, a renowned ski resort nestled in the Julian Alps, boasts well-groomed slopes suitable for all skill levels. Enjoy the thrill of gliding down the slopes surrounded by breathtaking alpine scenery, making it a perfect destination for winter sports enthusiasts.

8. Caving in Postojna Cave:

Explore the mesmerizing underground world of Postojna Cave, one of the most extensive cave systems in Europe. Embark on a guided tour and marvel at the stunning stalactites, stalagmites, and unique rock formations that have been shaped over millions of years. This adventure will leave you in awe of nature's wonders hidden beneath the surface.

9. Horseback Riding in Lipica:

Immerse yourself in Slovenia's equestrian heritage by horseback riding in Lipica, the birthplace of the world-famous Lipizzaner horses. Explore the picturesque countryside while riding these elegant and noble creatures, experiencing the bond between man and horse in a truly unique setting.

10. Kayaking in Lake Bohinj:

Discover the tranquility of Lake Bohinj, Slovenia's largest permanent lake, by kayaking through its serene waters. Paddle along the shoreline, surrounded by lush forests and towering mountains, and take in the beauty of this untouched natural paradise. This activity is perfect for nature lovers seeking a peaceful and immersive experience.

Slovenia's natural wonders and diverse landscapes provide an abundance of outdoor activities that cater to all adventure enthusiasts. Whether you're seeking adrenaline-pumping thrills or serene moments of tranquility, Slovenia has it all. Embark on these top 10 outdoor activities and let the beauty of this enchanting country captivate your heart and soul.

Chapter 23: Shopping in Slovenia

Introduction:

Welcome to Slovenia, a hidden gem in the heart of Europe that offers a delightful shopping experience for all visitors. From bustling markets to modern shopping centers, this chapter will guide you through the best places to shop in Slovenia and help you discover unique products to take home as souvenirs.

1. Ljubljana Central Market:

Located in the heart of the capital city, Ljubljana Central Market is a vibrant hub of activity. Here, you can find a wide array of fresh local produce, traditional Slovenian delicacies, and handmade crafts. Don't miss the chance to try some delicious honey and locally produced olive oil, which make for perfect gifts to bring back home.

2. BTC City, Ljubljana:

For those seeking a modern shopping experience, BTC City in Ljubljana is a must-visit destination. As one of Europe's largest shopping centers, it offers a plethora of international brands, trendy boutiques, and entertainment options. From fashion to electronics, you'll find everything you need under one roof.

3. Maribor's Old Vine House:

Maribor, Slovenia's second-largest city, is home to the oldest vine in the world. The Old Vine House, located in the city center, is a unique shopping destination where you can purchase exceptional wines made from this ancient vine. Take a piece of history back home and savor the flavors of Slovenia with every sip.

4. Piran's Artisan Shops:

Nestled on the Adriatic coast, the charming town of Piran is known for its rich artistic heritage. Explore the narrow streets and discover a myriad of artisan shops offering handmade ceramics, intricate lacework, and beautiful jewelry. These one-of-a-kind pieces make for unforgettable gifts or personal mementos.

5. Bohinj Dairy Farm:

Slovenia is renowned for its dairy products, and the Bohinj Dairy Farm is a place where you can witness the traditional cheese-making process firsthand. Located near Lake Bohinj, this farm offers a variety of locally produced cheeses, including the famous Bohinj cheese. Don't forget to taste some samples and choose your favorite to take home.

6. Idrija Lace Gallery:

Idrija, a town steeped in lace-making tradition, is home to the Idrija Lace Gallery. Here, you can admire delicate lace creations and even purchase unique lace products as souvenirs. From intricate tablecloths to elegant accessories, Idrija lace is a true symbol of Slovenian craftsmanship.

7. Koper's Antique Market:

If you have a passion for antiques and vintage treasures, Koper's Antique Market is the place to be. Located in the coastal town of Koper, this market offers a wide range of antique furniture, vintage clothing, and collectibles. Explore the stalls and uncover hidden gems that hold a piece of Slovenia's history.

Conclusion:

Shopping in Slovenia is a delightful experience that allows you to bring home a piece of this captivating country. Whether you choose to explore bustling markets, modern shopping centers, or artisan shops, you'll find unique products that reflect Slovenia's rich cultural heritage. From traditional delicacies to handmade crafts, these treasures will serve as reminders of your unforgettable Slovenian adventure. Happy shopping!

Chapter 24: Nightlife in Slovenia

Introduction:

Welcome to Chapter 24 of our tourist guide to Slovenia, where we explore the vibrant and exciting nightlife scene in this beautiful country. Slovenia may be known for its stunning natural landscapes and rich cultural heritage, but when the sun sets, a whole new world comes alive. From bustling cities to charming coastal towns, Slovenia offers a diverse range of options for those seeking an unforgettable night out. In this chapter, we will guide you through the best places to go and provide valuable tips for enjoying the nightlife in Slovenia.

1. Ljubljana - The Capital's Night Beat:

Ljubljana, the capital city of Slovenia, is undoubtedly the epicenter of the country's nightlife. As the sun dips below the horizon, the city's vibrant bars, clubs, and restaurants come to life. Start your evening with a stroll along the picturesque Ljubljanica River, lined with trendy bars and cafes. For a taste of local craft beer, head to Pivnica Union, a popular brewery with a lively atmosphere. If you're looking for a night of dancing, clubs like Cirkus and Top Six Club will keep you grooving until the early hours.

2. Maribor - Wine and Dine:

Located in the heart of Slovenia's wine-growing region, Maribor offers a unique nightlife experience centered around wine and culinary delights. Begin your evening with a visit to one of the city's wine bars, such as Vinoteka Sodček, where you can sample a variety of local wines. For a more refined experience, book a table at one of Maribor's top-notch restaurants, such as Mak, where you can indulge in exquisite Slovenian cuisine paired with exceptional wines. After dinner, head to Jazz Klub Satchmo for live music performances that will make your night unforgettable.

3. Piran - Coastal Charms After Dark:

Piran, a charming coastal town nestled on the Adriatic Sea, offers a unique blend of history, culture, and nightlife. As the sun sets, the town's narrow streets come alive with a vibrant atmosphere. Start your evening by savoring fresh seafood at one of the local restaurants along the waterfront. For a taste of local spirits, visit Piran's distillery, where you can try traditional Slovenian liqueurs. As the night progresses, head to Tartini Square, where you can enjoy live music performances and mingle with locals and fellow travelers.

4. Bled - Lakeside Serenity:

While Bled is known for its picturesque lake and stunning castle, it also offers a tranquil and enchanting nightlife experience. Begin your evening with a leisurely stroll around Lake Bled, taking in the serene atmosphere as the moon reflects on the water. For a romantic night out, book a table at Vila Bled Restaurant, where you can savor gourmet cuisine while enjoying breathtaking views of the lake. If you're in the mood for live music, Jazz Club Lovec is the place to be, offering an intimate setting with talented local musicians.

Tips for Enjoying the Nightlife in Slovenia:

1. Dress to impress: Slovenians tend to dress up for a night out, so make an effort to look stylish and presentable.

2. Plan your transportation: Public transportation may have limited schedules at night, so it's advisable to arrange alternative transportation in advance, such as taxis or ride-sharing services.

3. Embrace the local culture: Engage with locals, try traditional drinks and cuisine, and immerse yourself in the Slovenian way of life to enhance your nightlife experience.

4. Stay safe: As with any nightlife scene, it's essential to stay vigilant and aware of your surroundings. Stick to well-lit areas and avoid excessive alcohol consumption.

Conclusion:

As we conclude Chapter 24 of our tourist guide to Slovenia, we hope you're excited to explore the country's vibrant nightlife scene. Whether you prefer dancing the night away in Ljubljana, indulging in wine and culinary delights in Maribor, experiencing the coastal charms of Piran, or enjoying lakeside serenity in Bled, Slovenia offers something for every night owl. Remember to embrace the local culture, stay safe, and create unforgettable memories as you immerse yourself in the vibrant nightlife of this enchanting country.

Chapter 25: Festivals and Events in Slovenia

Slovenia, a hidden gem in the heart of Europe, offers a vibrant calendar of festivals and events throughout the year. From traditional folklore celebrations to contemporary music festivals, this chapter will guide you through the rich tapestry of cultural experiences that await you in Slovenia.

1. Maribor Theatre Festival (June)

Kicking off the summer season, the Maribor Theatre Festival showcases the best of Slovenian and international theatre. Renowned actors, directors, and playwrights come together to present captivating performances, pushing the boundaries of artistic expression.

2. Ljubljana Summer Festival (July - August)

Immerse yourself in the enchanting atmosphere of the Ljubljana Summer Festival. This month-long extravaganza features a diverse program of music, dance, theatre, and visual arts. From classical concerts in historic venues to open-air film screenings, there's something for everyone to enjoy.

3. Pivo in Cvetje (Beer and Flowers) Festival (August)

Raise your glass and celebrate the Pivo in Cvetje Festival in the charming town of Laško. This unique event combines the love for beer and the beauty of flowers, creating a lively atmosphere filled with music, dancing, and delicious culinary delights.

4. Ptuj Carnival (February)

Experience the vibrant spirit of Slovenia's largest carnival celebration in Ptuj. Dating back to pagan times, this colorful event features elaborate costumes, parades, and traditional rituals. Join the locals in embracing the festive atmosphere and let your imagination run wild.

5. Maribor Wine Festival (November)

Indulge in the rich flavors of Slovenian wines at the Maribor Wine Festival. Held in the country's second-largest city, this event brings together wine enthusiasts, sommeliers, and vineyard owners. Sample a wide variety of local wines, learn about the winemaking process, and discover the unique characteristics of Slovenia's wine regions.

6. Trnfest (August)

For a taste of alternative culture, head to Ljubljana's Trnfest. This grassroots festival showcases independent artists, musicians, and performers in a laid-back, bohemian atmosphere. From experimental theater to underground music gigs, Trnfest offers a platform for emerging talent and a chance to experience Slovenia's vibrant subculture.

7. Bled Days (July)

Bled, with its stunning lake and charming island, comes alive during Bled Days. This annual event celebrates the town's rich history and natural beauty through a series of cultural performances, sports competitions, and traditional crafts exhibitions. Don't miss the spectacular fireworks display reflecting on the serene waters of Lake Bled.

8. Planica Ski Jumping World Cup (March)

Witness the thrill and excitement of ski jumping at the Planica Ski Jumping World Cup. Held in the picturesque Planica Valley, this event attracts top athletes from around the globe. Marvel at their gravity-defying leaps and experience the electric atmosphere as the crowd cheers on their favorites.

9. Piran Musical Evenings (July - August)

Immerse yourself in the enchanting melodies of classical music at the Piran Musical Evenings. This prestigious festival takes place in the charming coastal town of Piran, where renowned musicians and orchestras deliver captivating performances against the backdrop of the Adriatic Sea.

10. Dragon Carnival (March)

Unleash your inner mythical creature at the Dragon Carnival in Ljubljana. Inspired by the city's iconic dragon statues, this lively event features elaborate costumes, street performances, and a grand parade. Join the revelers as they dance through the streets, bringing joy and merriment to all.

As you explore Slovenia, make sure to check the local tourism websites and event calendars for the most up-to-date information on festivals and events. Embrace the country's rich cultural heritage and create unforgettable memories as you immerse yourself in the vibrant tapestry of Slovenian celebrations.

Chapter 26: Activities for Couples in Slovenia

Introduction:

Slovenia, a hidden gem nestled in the heart of Europe, offers a plethora of romantic activities for couples seeking to create lasting memories. From breathtaking natural landscapes to charming cities, this enchanting country provides the perfect backdrop for an unforgettable romantic getaway. In this chapter, we will explore the top 10 most romantic activities for couples in Slovenia, showcasing the unique experiences that await you and your loved one.

1. Stroll Through Ljubljana's Old Town:

Begin your romantic journey in the capital city of Ljubljana, where the charming Old Town invites couples to wander hand in hand. Lose yourselves in the narrow cobblestone streets, admire the colorful Baroque architecture, and indulge in cozy cafés and intimate restaurants along the Ljubljanica River.

2. Discover the Fairytale Beauty of Lake Bled:

Embark on a romantic escapade to Lake Bled, a picturesque emerald-green lake adorned with a fairytale island and a medieval castle perched on a hilltop. Take a leisurely boat ride to the island, ring the Wishing Bell together, and savor a slice of the famous Bled cream cake at a lakeside café.

3. Unwind in the Thermal Springs of Rogaška Slatina:

For a truly relaxing experience, visit Rogaška Slatina, renowned for its healing thermal springs. Indulge in a couple's spa treatment, soak in the rejuvenating mineral waters, and let the tranquility of this enchanting spa town wash away your worries.

4. Explore the Romantic Predjama Castle:

Venture into the depths of the Slovenian countryside to discover the Predjama Castle, a medieval fortress built within a cave. Hold hands as you explore the castle's hidden passages, marvel at its impressive architecture, and imagine the romantic stories that unfolded within its walls.

5. Wander the Vineyards of Maribor:

The city of Maribor, nestled in the heart of Slovenia's wine-growing region, offers a romantic escape for wine-loving couples. Take a leisurely stroll through the lush vineyards, visit local wineries, and indulge in wine tastings, savoring the rich flavors of the region's finest vintages.

6. Experience the Magic of Postojna Cave:

Embark on a mesmerizing underground adventure in the Postojna Cave, one of the largest karst caves in Europe. Hand in hand, marvel at the stunning stalactite formations, board a unique cave train, and revel in the ethereal beauty of this subterranean wonderland.

7. Take a Romantic Hike in Triglav National Park:

For nature-loving couples, a romantic hike in Triglav National Park is a must. Explore pristine alpine valleys, crystal-clear lakes, and majestic waterfalls as you traverse the park's well-marked trails, immersing yourselves in the breathtaking beauty of Slovenia's highest peaks.

8. Enjoy a Sunset at Piran's Seaside Promenade:

Escape to the coastal town of Piran, where the Adriatic Sea meets the charming Mediterranean architecture. Walk hand in hand along the seaside promenade, savor a romantic dinner with a view, and witness the sun setting over the horizon, painting the sky in vibrant hues of orange and pink.

9. Embark on a Romantic Horse-Drawn Carriage Ride in Lipica:

Experience a fairytale-like moment in Lipica, the birthplace of the world-famous Lipizzaner horses. Climb aboard a horse-drawn carriage with your beloved, explore the idyllic countryside, and revel in the elegance and grace of these magnificent creatures.

10. Relax in the Alpine Paradise of Lake Bohinj:

Conclude your romantic journey in the tranquil embrace of Lake Bohinj, a hidden alpine gem surrounded by towering mountains. Rent a rowboat, paddle across the serene lake, and bask in the serenity of nature, creating lasting memories of your time together.

Conclusion:

Slovenia, with its diverse landscapes and enchanting cities, offers an array of romantic activities for couples seeking to ignite their love and create cherished moments. Whether you prefer exploring ancient castles, wandering through vineyards, or immersing yourselves in nature's embrace, Slovenia beckons you to embark on a romantic adventure like no other. Allow this chapter to guide you in discovering the top 10 most romantic activities for couples in Slovenia, and let the magic of this captivating country weave its spell on your hearts.

Chapter 27: Activities for Solo Travelers in Slovenia

Introduction:

Slovenia, a hidden gem nestled in the heart of Europe, offers a plethora of activities for solo travelers seeking adventure, cultural immersion, and personal growth. With its diverse landscapes, charming cities, and warm-hearted locals, Slovenia is an ideal destination for those who prefer to explore the world on their own terms. In this chapter, we will explore the top 10 activities that will make your solo trip to Slovenia an unforgettable experience.

1. Hiking in Triglav National Park:

Embark on a solo hiking adventure in Triglav National Park, Slovenia's only national park. With its stunning alpine scenery, crystal-clear lakes, and majestic peaks, this UNESCO World Heritage site offers a multitude of hiking trails suitable for all levels of experience. Whether you choose to conquer Mount Triglav, the highest peak in Slovenia, or opt for a more leisurely hike around Lake Bohinj, the solitude and serenity of nature will undoubtedly rejuvenate your soul.

2. Exploring Ljubljana:

Spend a day wandering through the charming streets of Ljubljana, Slovenia's capital city. As a solo traveler, you'll have the freedom to soak up the city's vibrant atmosphere at your own pace. Visit the iconic Ljubljana Castle for panoramic views, stroll along the Ljubljanica River, and indulge in the local cuisine at one of the many riverside cafes. Don't miss the chance to join a free walking tour to learn about the city's rich history and culture while meeting fellow travelers along the way.

3. Rafting on the Soča River:

For adrenaline junkies seeking an exhilarating experience, white-water rafting on the emerald-green Soča River is a must. The Soča Valley, often referred to as the adrenaline capital of Slovenia offers solo travelers the opportunity to navigate through thrilling rapids while surrounded by breathtaking alpine scenery. With experienced guides leading the way, you can rest assured that your safety is in good hands.

4. Wine Tasting in the Brda Region:

Indulge in Slovenia's vibrant wine culture by embarking on a solo wine-tasting adventure in the picturesque Brda region. Known as the Tuscany of Slovenia this wine-growing region boasts rolling hills covered in vineyards, charming villages, and wineries offering exquisite local wines. Sample a variety of wines, meet passionate winemakers, and learn about the region's winemaking traditions. Cheers to new discoveries and delightful flavors!

5. Caving in Postojna Cave:

Unleash your inner explorer by venturing into the mesmerizing underground world of Postojna Cave. As one of the world's largest karst cave systems, Postojna Cave offers a unique solo adventure filled with awe-inspiring stalactites, stalagmites, and underground chambers. Hop on a train that takes you deep into the cave, and then continue your exploration on foot, accompanied by knowledgeable guides who will reveal the secrets of this natural wonder.

6. Paragliding in the Julian Alps:

Take to the skies and experience the thrill of paragliding in the Julian Alps. With its breathtaking landscapes and favorable weather conditions, Slovenia is a paradise for paragliding enthusiasts. Soar above the picturesque alpine valleys, feel the wind in your hair, and enjoy the freedom of flight. Professional instructors will ensure your safety and guide you through this unforgettable solo adventure.

7. Cycling along the Parenzana Trail:

Embark on a solo cycling journey along the Parenzana Trail, a former railway line that now serves as a scenic route connecting

Slovenia, Italy, and Croatia. Pedal through charming villages, vineyards, and olive groves, while immersing yourself in the rich history and cultural heritage of the region. With well-marked trails and bike rental services available, solo travelers can explore this beautiful trail at their own pace.

8. Discovering Lake Bled:

No visit to Slovenia would be complete without exploring the enchanting beauty of Lake Bled. As a solo traveler, you can take your time to soak in the tranquility and serenity of this idyllic location. Rent a traditional wooden boat known as a pletna and row to the island in the middle of the lake, where you can climb the 99 steps to the Assumption of Mary Church. Alternatively, hike up to Bled Castle for panoramic views of the lake and surrounding mountains.

9. Volunteering on Organic Farms:

Embrace sustainable travel and immerse yourself in Slovenia's rural life by volunteering on organic farms. As a solo traveler, this unique opportunity allows you to connect with nature, learn about organic farming practices, and contribute to the local community. From picking fruits and vegetables to helping with animal care, you'll gain valuable insights into Slovenia's agricultural traditions while forging meaningful connections with locals and fellow volunteers.

10. Relaxing in the Thermal Spas:

Treat yourself to a solo wellness retreat by indulging in Slovenia's thermal spas. With numerous natural thermal springs scattered throughout the country, you can rejuvenate your body and mind in healing mineral-rich waters. Whether you choose to unwind in Terme Olimia, Terme Čatež, or Rogaška Slatina, these thermal spas offer a range of wellness treatments, saunas, and relaxation areas where you can unwind and find inner peace.

Conclusion:

Slovenia offers a myriad of activities for solo travelers, allowing you to create your own unique adventure while immersing yourself in the country's natural beauty, culture, and warm hospitality. From hiking in Triglav National Park to exploring the charming streets of Ljubljana, and from adrenaline-pumping activities to serene moments of relaxation, Slovenia has something to offer every solo traveler seeking an unforgettable journey of self-discovery. So pack your bags, embrace the freedom of solo travel, and embark on a Slovenian adventure like no other.

Chapter 28: Budget-friendly activities in Slovenia

Introduction:

Welcome to Slovenia, a hidden gem in the heart of Europe that offers a plethora of budget-friendly activities for every type of traveler. From breathtaking natural landscapes to charming towns and cities, Slovenia has something to suit every taste and budget. In this chapter, we will explore the top 10 budget-friendly activities that will allow you to make the most of your visit without breaking the bank.

1. Explore Ljubljana's Old Town:

Start your budget-friendly adventure in Slovenia by exploring the charming streets of Ljubljana's Old Town. Wander through the narrow cobblestone alleys, admire the colorful buildings, and soak in the vibrant atmosphere of this picturesque capital city. Don't forget to visit the iconic Ljubljana Castle, which offers stunning panoramic views of the city and is accessible for free.

2. Discover Lake Bled:

No visit to Slovenia is complete without a trip to Lake Bled. This enchanting lake, with its emerald-green water and a fairytale-like island in the middle, is a must-see attraction. Take a leisurely stroll around the lake, rent a rowboat to reach the island, or hike up to the Bled Castle for breathtaking views. Entrance to the lake and its surroundings is free, allowing you to enjoy its beauty without spending a fortune.

3. Hike in Triglav National Park:

For nature enthusiasts on a budget, Triglav National Park is a paradise waiting to be explored. Lace up your hiking boots and embark on one of the many scenic trails that wind through this pristine wilderness. From cascading waterfalls to majestic peaks, Triglav National Park offers unparalleled beauty without the need for pricey guided tours.

4. Visit Predjama Castle:

Step back in time and explore the fascinating Predjama Castle, perched dramatically on a cliffside. This medieval marvel is a sight to behold and can be explored at an affordable price. Wander through its hidden chambers, secret tunnels, and learn about the castle's intriguing history. Don't miss the opportunity to visit the nearby Postojna Cave, one of the world's largest cave systems, which offers discounted combination tickets.

5. Relax in the Thermal Spas:

Slovenia is known for its thermal spas, which offer a perfect way to relax and rejuvenate without breaking the bank. Visit Terme Čatež, Terme Olimia, or Terme Dobrna, among others, and indulge in the healing properties of thermal waters. Enjoy a range of affordable spa treatments, soak in the warm pools, and let your worries melt away in these budget-friendly havens of tranquility.

6. Taste Slovenian Cuisine:

Exploring a country's culinary delights doesn't have to be expensive. In Slovenia, you can savor traditional dishes without emptying your wallet. Visit local markets, such as Ljubljana Central Market, and sample delicious street food like burek or štruklji. Alternatively, dine at local taverns and try hearty dishes like potica or kranjska klobasa, which offer excellent value for money.

7. Cycle along the Parenzana Trail:

For outdoor enthusiasts, the Parenzana Trail offers an unforgettable experience. This former railway line has been transformed into a scenic cycling route that spans through Slovenia, Croatia, and Italy. Rent a bike and pedal through picturesque landscapes, charming villages, and vineyards, all while enjoying the fresh air and stunning views. Cycling along the Parenzana Trail is an affordable and eco-friendly way to explore the region.

8. Discover the Skocjan Caves:

Marvel at the wonders of the underground world by visiting the Skocjan Caves, a UNESCO World Heritage site. Explore the vast chambers, awe-inspiring stalactites, and an underground river that has carved its way through the limestone over millions of years. Guided tours are available at reasonable prices, allowing you to witness the mesmerizing beauty of this natural wonder without breaking your budget.

9. Enjoy Lake Bohinj:

Escape the crowds and head to Lake Bohinj, a tranquil oasis nestled in the Julian Alps. Surrounded by lush forests and majestic mountains, this pristine lake offers endless opportunities for relaxation and outdoor activities. Swim in its crystal-clear waters, hike along its scenic trails, or simply bask in the serenity of nature. Entrance to the lake and most of its surroundings is free, making it an ideal budget-friendly destination.

10. Attend Festivals and Events:

Immerse yourself in Slovenian culture by attending various festivals and events that take place throughout the year. From music festivals to traditional folklore celebrations, there is always something happening in Slovenia. Many of these events offer free or affordable admission, allowing you to experience the country's vibrant cultural scene without straining your budget.

Conclusion:

Slovenia is a country that caters to travelers on all budgets. By exploring these top 10 budget-friendly activities, you can make the most of your visit to this stunning destination without breaking the bank. From natural wonders to cultural experiences, Slovenia has it all, ensuring an unforgettable adventure that won't empty your wallet.

Chapter 29: Off-the-Beaten-Path Activities in Slovenia

Welcome to the hidden gems of Slovenia! In this chapter, we will take you on a journey through the lesser-known, off-the-beaten-path activities that this enchanting country has to offer. While Slovenia is famous for its stunning landscapes and charming cities, there are numerous unique experiences awaiting those who venture off the tourist trail. Get ready to discover the authentic and extraordinary side of Slovenia with our top 10 off-the-beaten-path activities.

1. Explore the Underground Wonders of Postojna Cave

Escape the crowds and descend into the mesmerizing underground world of Postojna Cave. Embark on a guided tour through its labyrinthine passages, marvel at the stunning stalactite formations, and encounter the mysterious olm, a rare cave-dwelling amphibian.

2. Wander Through the Fairytale-like Town of Ptuj

Step into a fairytale as you explore the charming town of Ptuj. Wander through its narrow medieval streets, visit the majestic Ptuj Castle, and immerse yourself in the rich history and culture of this hidden gem.

3. Discover the Natural Beauty of Lake Bohinj

While Lake Bled often steals the spotlight, venture to the lesser-known Lake Bohinj for a tranquil escape amidst breathtaking alpine scenery. Take a leisurely boat ride, hike through pristine forests, or simply relax by the peaceful lakeshore.

4. Uncover the Mysteries of Predjama Castle

Perched dramatically in the mouth of a cave, Predjama Castle is a sight to behold. Explore its hidden chambers, learn about the legendary knight Erazem, and marvel at the castle's architectural marvels.

5. Indulge in the Culinary Delights of Kobarid

Slovenia's gastronomy extends far beyond its capital city. Visit the charming town of Kobarid, renowned for its culinary delights. Savor traditional dishes, such as the mouthwatering Kobarid dumplings, and experience the true flavors of Slovenian cuisine.

6. Trek to the Summit of Triglav

For the adventurous souls seeking a challenge, embark on a journey to the summit of Mount Triglav, the highest peak in Slovenia. Traverse rugged landscapes, conquer steep trails, and be rewarded with breathtaking panoramic views from the top.

7. Immerse Yourself in the Traditional Village Life of Velika Planina

Step back in time as you visit the idyllic alpine village of Velika Planina. Experience the traditional way of life, admire the unique architecture of herdsmen's huts, and enjoy the tranquility of this hidden mountain paradise.

8. Explore the Enchanting Škocjan Caves

Venture into the depths of the Škocjan Caves, a UNESCO World Heritage site. Marvel at the colossal underground chambers, cross the dramatic suspended bridge, and witness the awe-inspiring power of the Reka River as it carves its way through the limestone.

9. Embark on a Cycling Adventure in the Soča Valley

Discover the pristine beauty of the Soča Valley on two wheels. Cycle along the emerald Soča River, pass through picturesque villages, and soak in the breathtaking alpine scenery that surrounds you.

10. Relax in the Thermal Springs of Dobrna

Escape the hustle and bustle of city life and unwind in the healing thermal springs of Dobrna. Immerse yourself in the rejuvenating waters, indulge in spa treatments, and experience the ultimate relaxation in this hidden oasis.

These off-the-beaten-path activities are just a glimpse of the countless unique experiences that await you in Slovenia. So, step away from the well-trodden path and embrace the extraordinary. Slovenia's hidden treasures are waiting to be discovered by the adventurous traveler.

Chapter 30: Sustainable Tourism Experiences in Slovenia

Introduction:

Slovenia, a hidden gem nestled in the heart of Europe, offers a plethora of sustainable tourism experiences that cater to the environmentally conscious traveler. From its untouched natural landscapes to its commitment to eco-friendly practices, Slovenia has emerged as a leading destination for sustainable tourism. In this chapter, we will explore the top 10 sustainable tourism experiences that highlight Slovenia's dedication to preserving its natural and cultural heritage.

1. Exploring Triglav National Park:

Triglav National Park, Slovenia's only national park, is a haven for outdoor enthusiasts seeking sustainable adventures. With its diverse ecosystems, including the Julian Alps, emerald lakes, and lush forests, visitors can engage in activities such as hiking, cycling, and wildlife spotting while respecting the park's preservation efforts.

2. Discovering Ljubljana's Green Initiatives:

Ljubljana, the capital city of Slovenia, has gained international recognition for its commitment to sustainability. Take a guided tour to learn about the city's green initiatives, such as waste management systems, pedestrian-only zones, and extensive cycling infrastructure. Visit the Ljubljana Botanical Garden, a hub for biodiversity conservation and research.

3. Sustainable Farm Stays in the Slovenian Countryside:

Escape the hustle and bustle of city life by staying at one of Slovenia's sustainable farms. Experience traditional Slovenian hospitality while supporting local farmers who prioritize organic farming practices and offer farm-to-table meals. Participate in farm activities, such as milking cows, harvesting fruits, or learning traditional crafts.

4. Wine Tasting in Vipava Valley:

The Vipava Valley, known for its vineyards and picturesque landscapes, offers a sustainable wine-tasting experience. Visit organic and biodynamic wineries that prioritize low-impact viticulture methods. Savor exquisite wines while learning about sustainable grape cultivation and the region's rich winemaking traditions.

5. Cycling along the Soča River:

Embark on a cycling adventure along the pristine Soča River, renowned for its turquoise waters and breathtaking scenery. Rent a bicycle from one of the eco-friendly rental shops and follow the well-maintained cycling paths that wind through the valley. Enjoy the serenity of nature while pedaling through charming villages and stopping at sustainable eateries along the way.

6. Exploring the Škocjan Caves:

The Škocjan Caves, a UNESCO World Heritage site, offer an awe-inspiring experience for nature enthusiasts. Take a guided tour through the underground labyrinth, marveling at the immense chambers, stalactites, and an underground river. Learn about the cave's fragile ecosystem and the ongoing conservation efforts to preserve this geological wonder.

7. Sustainable Skiing in Kranjska Gora:

Kranjska Gora, a popular winter destination, is committed to sustainable skiing practices. Enjoy the thrill of skiing or snowboarding on the well-maintained slopes while knowing that the resort prioritizes energy-efficient snowmaking, waste management, and environmental education programs. Explore the nearby Triglav National Park for additional winter activities.

8. Birdwatching at Lake Cerknica:

Lake Cerknica, a unique intermittent lake, is a paradise for birdwatchers. Visit the lake during the spring or autumn migration seasons to witness the spectacle of numerous bird species. Join a guided birdwatching tour led by knowledgeable local experts who emphasize the importance of protecting the lake's delicate ecosystem.

9. Eco-friendly Accommodation in Bohinj:

Bohinj, a tranquil alpine region, offers a range of eco-friendly accommodations that blend seamlessly with the natural surroundings. Stay in sustainable lodges, eco-hotels, or glamping sites that implement energy-saving measures and promote responsible tourism practices. Immerse yourself in the pristine nature of Lake Bohinj and the Triglav National Park.

10. Volunteering in the Karst Region:

Engage in sustainable tourism by participating in volunteer programs in the Karst region. Work alongside local conservation organizations to protect and restore the unique Karst landscape, including its underground caves, sinkholes, and rare species. Contribute to sustainable development initiatives while gaining a deeper understanding of Slovenia's natural heritage.

Conclusion:

Slovenia's commitment to sustainable tourism experiences is evident in its conservation efforts, eco-friendly accommodations, and promotion of responsible travel practices. By engaging in these top 10 sustainable tourism experiences, visitors can contribute to the preservation of Slovenia's natural and cultural treasures while creating unforgettable memories. Embark on a journey that combines adventure, education, and sustainability in this enchanting European destination.

Chapter 31: Responsible Tourism Experiences in Slovenia

Introduction:

Slovenia, a hidden gem in Central Europe, offers a plethora of responsible tourism experiences that allow visitors to explore the country's natural wonders while minimizing their environmental impact. In this chapter, we will delve into the top 10 responsible tourism experiences in Slovenia, highlighting the unique and truthful aspects that make them truly remarkable.

1. Discovering the Triglav National Park:

Triglav National Park, Slovenia's only national park, is a haven for nature enthusiasts. Visitors can engage in responsible activities such as hiking, cycling, and wildlife spotting while respecting the park's fragile ecosystems. Local guides provide insightful information about the park's biodiversity, emphasizing the importance of preserving this pristine environment.

2. Exploring the Ljubljana Marshes:

The Ljubljana Marshes, a wetland of international importance, offer a unique responsible tourism experience. Visitors can join guided tours that focus on the preservation of this delicate ecosystem. By learning about the marshes' flora and fauna, visitors gain a deeper understanding of the importance of conservation efforts.

3. Supporting Sustainable Wineries:

Slovenia's wine culture is deeply rooted in sustainable practices. Responsible tourists can visit organic and biodynamic wineries, where they can participate in wine tastings and learn about the environmentally friendly methods employed in the winemaking process. This experience not only supports local producers but also promotes responsible agricultural practices.

4. Engaging with Local Communities:

Responsible tourism in Slovenia extends beyond the natural environment. By engaging with local communities, visitors can gain insights into the country's rich cultural heritage. Participating in traditional workshops, festivals, and events not only supports local artisans but also fosters cross-cultural understanding and appreciation.

5. Volunteering in Nature Conservation Projects:

For those seeking a more hands-on experience, Slovenia offers various volunteering opportunities in nature conservation projects. From reforestation efforts to wildlife monitoring, responsible tourists can actively contribute to the preservation of Slovenia's natural habitats, leaving a positive impact on the environment.

6. Staying in Eco-Friendly Accommodations:

Slovenia boasts a wide range of eco-friendly accommodations, from sustainable hotels to eco-lodges nestled in the heart of nature. These establishments prioritize energy efficiency, waste reduction, and locally sourced products, allowing responsible tourists to enjoy their stay while minimizing their carbon footprint.

7. Exploring Sustainable Cuisine:

Slovenian cuisine is deeply rooted in sustainable practices, with many restaurants emphasizing locally sourced ingredients and traditional cooking methods. Responsible tourists can indulge in farm-to-table experiences, where they can savor authentic flavors while supporting local farmers and reducing their food miles.

8. Cycling the Julian Alps:

Slovenia's Julian Alps provide a breathtaking backdrop for responsible cycling adventures. Cyclists can explore the region's picturesque landscapes, while adhering to designated cycling paths and minimizing their impact on the environment. Local tour operators offer bike rentals and guided tours, ensuring a safe and responsible experience.

9. Participating in Responsible Fishing:

Slovenia's crystal-clear rivers and lakes offer excellent fishing opportunities. Responsible anglers can engage in catch-and-release practices, preserving fish populations and maintaining the ecological balance of these aquatic ecosystems. Local fishing guides provide education on responsible fishing techniques and the importance of conservation.

10. Supporting Local Conservation Initiatives:

Slovenia is home to numerous conservation initiatives aimed at preserving its natural and cultural heritage. Responsible tourists can contribute by donating to these initiatives or participating in fundraising events. By supporting these local initiatives, visitors actively contribute to the long-term sustainability of Slovenia's tourism industry.

Conclusion:

Slovenia's commitment to responsible tourism is evident through its diverse range of experiences that prioritize environmental and cultural conservation. By engaging in these top 10 responsible tourism experiences, visitors can explore Slovenia's natural wonders, support local communities, and leave a positive impact on the country's sustainability efforts.

Chapter 32: Volunteer Opportunities in Slovenia

Introduction:

Slovenia, a picturesque country nestled in the heart of Europe, is not only known for its stunning landscapes and rich cultural heritage but also for its commitment to social responsibility. For those seeking to make a positive impact while exploring this enchanting destination, there are numerous volunteer opportunities available. In this chapter, we will explore the top 10 volunteer opportunities in Slovenia, offering you a chance to contribute to the local community and create unforgettable memories.

1. Environmental Conservation:

Slovenia takes great pride in its pristine natural environment. Volunteer with local organizations dedicated to preserving and restoring the country's forests, rivers, and wildlife. Participate in tree planting initiatives, clean-up campaigns, or assist in monitoring endangered species, contributing to the long-term sustainability of Slovenia's unique ecosystems.

2. Cultural Heritage Preservation:

Immerse yourself in Slovenia's rich history and assist in the preservation of its cultural heritage. Join restoration projects in ancient castles, churches, and museums, helping to conserve these architectural treasures for future generations. Engage with local communities and learn traditional crafts, such as pottery or lace-making, while supporting local artisans.

3. Social Welfare:

Make a difference in the lives of vulnerable individuals by volunteering in social welfare programs. Collaborate with organizations that provide support to refugees, the elderly, or individuals with disabilities. Offer companionship, organize recreational activities, or contribute your skills in areas such as healthcare, education, or counseling.

4. Sustainable Agriculture:

Experience the beauty of rural Slovenia while volunteering in sustainable agriculture projects. Work alongside local farmers, learning organic farming techniques and promoting sustainable practices. Contribute to the production of local, organic food, participate in harvest festivals, and gain a deeper understanding of Slovenia's agrarian traditions.

5. Youth Empowerment:

Inspire and empower Slovenia's youth by volunteering in educational programs. Assist in after-school activities, mentor disadvantaged children, or organize workshops that promote creativity and critical thinking. Your involvement can help shape the future of the country by nurturing the potential of its young generation.

6. Animal Welfare:

For animal lovers, Slovenia offers various opportunities to contribute to the welfare of its furry inhabitants. Volunteer at animal shelters, assisting in the care and rehabilitation of abandoned or mistreated animals. Help raise awareness about responsible pet ownership and support initiatives aimed at reducing animal cruelty.

7. Sustainable Tourism:

Slovenia prides itself on its commitment to sustainable tourism. Get involved in projects that promote responsible travel and environmental awareness. Participate in trail maintenance, eco-tourism initiatives, or assist in organizing events that showcase the country's natural and cultural heritage, encouraging visitors to appreciate and protect Slovenia's pristine landscapes.

8. Community Development:

Engage with local communities and contribute to their development by volunteering in community-based projects. Collaborate with organizations that focus on improving infrastructure, revitalizing public spaces, or promoting cultural events. Your efforts will help foster a sense of pride and unity among Slovenia's diverse communities.

9. Education and Language Exchange:

Share your knowledge and language skills by volunteering in educational programs. Assist in teaching English or other subjects in schools, language centers, or community organizations. Engage in language exchanges with locals, promoting cultural understanding and fostering connections between different communities.

10. Emergency Response:

In times of crisis, lend a helping hand by joining emergency response teams. Volunteer with organizations that provide disaster relief, assisting in rescue operations, offering support to affected communities, and helping with reconstruction efforts. Your dedication and compassion can make a significant difference during challenging times.

Conclusion:

Slovenia's commitment to social responsibility and sustainability offers a plethora of volunteer opportunities for those who wish to make a positive impact while exploring this captivating country. Whether you choose to contribute to environmental conservation, cultural heritage preservation, social welfare, or any other field, your volunteer experience in Slovenia will be both rewarding and unforgettable. Embrace the chance to give back, immerse yourself in the local community, and create lasting memories while making a difference.

Chapter 33: Visas and Immigration Requirements for Slovenia

Introduction:

Welcome to Chapter 33 of our comprehensive tourist guide on Slovenia. In this chapter, we will provide you with essential information regarding visas and immigration requirements for visiting Slovenia. It is crucial to understand the necessary procedures and regulations to ensure a smooth and hassle-free entry into this beautiful country.

1. Visa-Free Entry:

Slovenia, being a member of the European Union and the Schengen Area, allows visa-free entry for citizens of many countries. If you are a citizen of the European Union, the European Economic Area, Switzerland, or hold a valid Schengen visa, you can enter Slovenia without requiring an additional visa. The duration of your stay is limited to 90 days within a 180-day period.

2. Visa Requirements:

For citizens of countries not mentioned in the visa-free entry section, a visa is required to enter Slovenia. To obtain a visa, you will need to visit the Slovenian embassy or consulate in your home country or the nearest Slovenian diplomatic mission. It is advisable to start the visa application process well in advance of your intended travel date.

3. Types of Visas:

Slovenia offers various types of visas depending on the purpose of your visit. The most common types include:

a. Schengen Visa: This visa allows you to travel to Slovenia and other Schengen countries. Depending on your purpose of visit, you can apply for a tourist visa, business visa, or other relevant categories. The Schengen visa is valid for a maximum of 90 days within a 180-day period.

b. National Visa: If your intended stay in Slovenia exceeds 90 days, you will need to apply for a national visa. This visa allows you to enter and reside in Slovenia for a specific purpose, such as work, study, or family reunification. The national visa must be obtained before your arrival in Slovenia.

4. Visa Application Process:

To apply for a visa, you will need to submit the following documents to the Slovenian embassy or consulate:

a. Completed visa application form

b. Valid passport with a minimum of six months' validity beyond your intended stay

c. Recent passport-sized photographs

d. Proof of travel insurance covering medical expenses and repatriation

e. Proof of accommodation in Slovenia

f. Proof of sufficient financial means to support yourself during your stay

g. Travel itinerary and return ticket

h. Proof of purpose of visit (e.g., invitation letter, business contacts, study enrollment, etc.)

i. Additional documents may be required depending on the type of visa you are applying for.

5. Immigration Requirements:

Upon arrival in Slovenia, you will need to go through immigration control at the port of entry. The immigration officer may ask for the following documents:

a. Valid passport

b. Visa (if applicable)

c. Proof of sufficient financial means

d. Proof of accommodation in Slovenia

e. Return ticket or onward travel itinerary

6. Extension of Stay:

If you wish to extend your stay beyond the permitted duration, you must apply for an extension at the Slovenian Administrative Unit before your current visa expires. Extensions are granted on a case-by-case basis and are subject to specific conditions.

Conclusion:

This concludes Chapter 33 of our tourist guide on Slovenia, focusing on visas and immigration requirements. We hope this information has provided you with a clear understanding of the necessary procedures to enter Slovenia legally. Remember to check the latest updates and regulations regarding visas and immigration requirements before planning your trip. Enjoy your visit to Slovenia!

Chapter 34: Money and Banking in Slovenia

Introduction:

Welcome to Slovenia, a country known for its stunning landscapes, rich cultural heritage, and warm hospitality. As you embark on your journey through this enchanting land, it is essential to familiarize yourself with the local currency, exchange rates, ATMs, and credit card usage. This chapter will provide you with valuable insights into money and banking in Slovenia, ensuring a seamless and hassle-free experience during your visit.

The Slovenian Currency:

The official currency of Slovenia is the Euro (€), which replaced the Slovenian Tolar in 2007. As a member of the Eurozone, Slovenia adopted the Euro as its sole legal tender. This means that you will not need to exchange your currency upon arrival, making transactions and budgeting more convenient during your stay.

Exchange Rates:

Exchange rates fluctuate daily, influenced by various economic factors. To ensure you get the most favorable rates, it is advisable to exchange your currency at official exchange offices or banks. These establishments are widely available throughout Slovenia, particularly in major cities and tourist areas. Avoid exchanging money at unauthorized locations, as they may charge higher fees or offer unfavorable rates.

ATMs and Credit Cards:

Slovenia boasts a well-developed banking infrastructure, making it easy to access your funds through ATMs. ATMs are widely available in urban areas, including airports, train stations, and shopping centers. Most ATMs accept major international debit and credit cards, such as Visa and Mastercard. However, it is always prudent to inform your bank of your travel plans to ensure uninterrupted card usage.

Credit cards are widely accepted in hotels, restaurants, and larger retail establishments. However, it is advisable to carry some cash for smaller businesses, markets, and rural areas where card acceptance may be limited. When using your credit card, be cautious of potential skimming devices and always keep your card in sight during transactions to prevent any unauthorized use.

Banking Hours and Services:

Banking hours in Slovenia typically follow a standard schedule, operating from Monday to Friday, between 8:30 am and 4:30 pm. Some banks may offer limited services on Saturdays, while others remain closed. It is advisable to check the specific operating hours of your bank or consult with your hotel concierge for alternative banking options during weekends or public holidays.

Banks in Slovenia provide a wide range of services, including currency exchange, money transfers, and cashing traveler's checks. It is worth noting that traveler's checks are not as widely accepted as they once were, so it is advisable to carry a mix of cash and cards for convenience.

Safety and Security:

Slovenia is generally a safe country for tourists, and incidents of theft or fraud are relatively low. However, it is always prudent to exercise caution and take necessary precautions. Keep your money and valuables secure, avoid displaying large sums of cash in public, and use ATMs located in well-lit and populated areas. If you encounter any issues with your credit card or suspect fraudulent activity, contact your bank immediately to report the incident.

Conclusion:

Understanding the currency, exchange rates, ATMs, and credit card usage in Slovenia is crucial for a smooth and enjoyable travel experience. By familiarizing yourself with the information provided in this chapter, you are well-equipped to handle financial matters confidently during your stay. Embrace the beauty of Slovenia while knowing that your money is secure and accessible whenever you need it.

Chapter 35: Communication in Slovenia

Introduction:

Slovenia, a picturesque country nestled in the heart of Europe, offers a seamless communication experience to both its residents and visitors. This chapter will provide you with an overview of the phone system, internet access, and postal service in Slovenia, ensuring that you stay connected throughout your adventures in this captivating nation.

1. The Phone System:

Slovenia boasts a modern and reliable phone system, allowing tourists to easily stay in touch with loved ones or navigate their way through the country. The country code for Slovenia is +386, and it is important to note that international calls can be quite expensive. To avoid exorbitant charges, it is recommended to purchase a local SIM card, readily available at various mobile network providers.

2. Internet Access:

Slovenia takes pride in its advanced telecommunications infrastructure, ensuring excellent internet connectivity throughout the country. Most hotels, restaurants, cafes, and public spaces offer free Wi-Fi access, allowing visitors to stay connected while exploring Slovenia's breathtaking landscapes. Additionally, internet cafes are scattered across major cities, providing affordable access to those who may not have their own devices.

3. Postal Service:

The Slovenian postal service, known as Pošta Slovenije, is renowned for its efficiency and reliability. With a vast network of post offices across the country, sending and receiving mail is a hassle-free experience. Post offices can be easily identified by the recognizable yellow and blue signage. It is important to note that postage rates may vary depending on the weight and destination of your mail, so it is advisable to inquire about the costs before sending any packages.

4. Mobile Communication and Roaming:

For travelers who prefer to use their own mobile phones, Slovenia offers excellent network coverage. Roaming services are available for many international carriers, but it is essential to check with your provider regarding potential additional charges. To avoid unexpected fees, purchasing a local SIM card is recommended, enabling you to enjoy affordable local rates for calls, texts, and data usage.

5. Emergency Services:

In case of any emergencies during your time in Slovenia, it is crucial to be aware of the local emergency numbers. The general emergency number is 112, which connects you to police, ambulance, and fire services. English-speaking operators are available to assist you, ensuring prompt and efficient communication during critical situations.

Conclusion:

Communication in Slovenia is a seamless experience, with a modern phone system, widespread internet access, and a reliable postal service. Whether you need to connect with loved ones, share your adventures on social media, or send postcards to friends back home, Slovenia's communication infrastructure has got you covered. Stay connected, explore with ease, and enjoy your time in this enchanting country.

Chapter 36: Health and Safety in Slovenia

Introduction:

Welcome to Chapter 36 of our tourist guide, where we will provide you with essential information regarding health and safety in Slovenia. Ensuring a safe and healthy trip is crucial for an enjoyable experience, and we aim to equip you with the knowledge needed to make informed decisions during your visit. From common health risks to safety tips, this chapter will assist you in having a worry-free journey through Slovenia.

1. Healthcare System:

Slovenia boasts a well-developed healthcare system, ensuring quality medical care for both residents and visitors. Public healthcare facilities are easily accessible throughout the country, with hospitals and clinics equipped with modern facilities and skilled medical professionals. Private healthcare options are also available, offering a higher level of personalized care for those who prefer it.

2. Common Health Risks:

a) Tick-Borne Encephalitis (TBE): Slovenia has reported cases of tick-borne encephalitis, particularly in forested areas. If you plan on hiking or exploring rural regions, consider getting vaccinated and taking precautions such as wearing long sleeves, using insect repellent, and checking for ticks regularly.

b) Sunburn and Heatstroke: During the summer months, Slovenia experiences high temperatures. Protect yourself from the sun by wearing sunscreen, hats, and sunglasses, and stay hydrated to prevent heat-related illnesses.

c) Water Safety: Slovenia's lakes and rivers offer opportunities for swimming and water activities. However, be cautious of strong currents, follow safety guidelines, and only swim in designated areas to avoid accidents.

3. Medical Insurance:

It is strongly recommended to have comprehensive travel insurance that covers medical expenses while in Slovenia. Check with your insurance provider to ensure your policy includes coverage for emergency medical evacuation, as well as any specific activities you plan to engage in, such as hiking or water sports.

4. Prescription Medications:

If you require prescription medications, ensure you have an ample supply for the duration of your stay. Carry them in their original packaging, along with a copy of the prescription or a letter from your healthcare provider, as customs may require documentation.

5. Emergency Services:

In case of an emergency, dial 112, Slovenia's universal emergency number. Operators are trained to assist in medical emergencies, accidents, and other urgent situations. English-speaking operators are available, making it easier to communicate your needs.

6. Food and Water Safety:

Slovenia maintains high standards of food safety. However, it is advisable to consume food from reputable establishments and ensure that it is properly cooked and served. Tap water in Slovenia is generally safe to drink, but if you prefer, bottled water is widely available.

7. Personal Safety:

Slovenia is generally a safe country to visit, with low crime rates. However, it is always wise to take precautions to protect yourself and your belongings. Avoid displaying valuable items openly, be cautious in crowded areas, and use lockers or hotel safes to secure your belongings.

Conclusion:

As you embark on your journey through Slovenia, remember that prioritizing your health and safety is essential for a memorable trip. By being aware of common health risks, taking necessary precautions, and staying informed, you can fully enjoy the beauty and charm of this remarkable country. Stay safe, take care of yourself, and make the most of your Slovenian adventure!

Chapter 37: Travel Insurance for Slovenia

Introduction:

When planning your trip to Slovenia, it is essential to consider travel insurance as a vital component of your travel arrangements. Travel insurance provides financial protection and peace of mind, ensuring that you are prepared for any unforeseen circumstances that may arise during your visit to this enchanting country. In this chapter, we will explore the benefits of travel insurance and guide you on how to purchase the most suitable policy for your Slovenian adventure.

Benefits of Travel Insurance:

1. Medical Expenses Coverage: One of the primary benefits of travel insurance is the coverage it provides for medical expenses. In Slovenia, travel insurance can help cover the costs of emergency medical treatment, hospitalization, and even medical evacuation if necessary. With travel insurance, you can explore Slovenia with confidence, knowing that you are protected in case of any unexpected medical emergencies.

2. Trip Cancellation or Interruption Coverage: Travel plans can sometimes be disrupted due to unforeseen circumstances such as illness, injury, or natural disasters. Travel insurance can safeguard your investment by reimbursing you for non-refundable expenses, such as flights, accommodation, and tour bookings, in case you need to cancel or cut short your trip to Slovenia.

3. Lost or Delayed Baggage Coverage: Imagine arriving in Slovenia, only to realize that your luggage has been lost or delayed. Travel insurance can provide coverage for the replacement of essential items, such as clothing and toiletries, until your baggage is recovered or replaced. This benefit ensures that you can continue your journey without unnecessary inconvenience.

4. Personal Liability Coverage: Accidents can happen even when you are on vacation. In the unfortunate event that you cause damage to

property or injure someone while in Slovenia, travel insurance can offer personal liability coverage. This coverage can help protect you from potential legal expenses and give you peace of mind during your stay.

How to Purchase Travel Insurance for Slovenia:

1. Research and Compare Policies: Start by researching reputable travel insurance providers that offer coverage specifically for Slovenia. Compare the policies they offer, ensuring they include the benefits mentioned above and any additional coverage you may require.

2. Assess Your Needs: Consider the nature of your trip, the duration of your stay, and the activities you plan to engage in while in Slovenia. This assessment will help you determine the level of coverage you need and any additional add-ons that might be beneficial, such as adventure sports coverage or rental car insurance.

3. Read the Policy Details Carefully: Before purchasing a travel insurance policy, carefully read the policy wording and terms and conditions. Pay attention to coverage limits, exclusions, and any pre-existing medical conditions that may affect your coverage.

4. Seek Expert Advice: If you are unsure about any aspect of the policy or need assistance in selecting the most suitable coverage, consider consulting with a travel insurance specialist or insurance broker. They can provide guidance tailored to your specific needs and help you make an informed decision.

5. Purchase Early: It is advisable to purchase travel insurance as soon as you have made your initial travel arrangements. This ensures that you are covered for any unexpected events that may occur before your departure, such as illness or trip cancellation.

Conclusion:

Travel insurance is an essential investment when planning your trip to Slovenia. It provides financial protection and peace of mind, allowing you to fully immerse yourself in the country's natural beauty, rich culture, and vibrant cities. By researching, assessing your needs, and purchasing a suitable policy, you can explore Slovenia with confidence, knowing that you are prepared for any unforeseen circumstances that may arise during your journey.

Chapter 38: Learning the Language of Slovenia

Introduction:

Slovenia, a charming country nestled in the heart of Europe, boasts a rich cultural heritage and breathtaking natural landscapes. To truly immerse yourself in the Slovenian experience, learning the local language can be immensely rewarding. In this chapter, we will explore the resources available for learning the language of Slovenia, enabling you to communicate with locals, understand the country's history, and appreciate its vibrant culture.

1. Language Schools:

Slovenia is home to numerous language schools that cater to both beginners and advanced learners. These institutions offer a structured curriculum, experienced teachers, and immersive learning experiences. The courses cover essential aspects of the Slovenian language, including grammar, vocabulary, pronunciation, and cultural nuances. Some reputable language schools in Slovenia include the University of Ljubljana Language Centre, the Centre for Slovene as a Second and Foreign Language, and the Slovene Learning Online platform.

2. Online Resources:

In the digital age, learning a new language has become more accessible than ever. Various online platforms provide comprehensive Slovenian language courses, interactive exercises, and multimedia resources. Websites like Duolingo, Memrise, and Babbel offer -friendly interfaces and engaging lessons, making language learning an enjoyable experience. Additionally, YouTube channels such as Learn Slovenian with Ivana and Slovenian Lessons provide free video tutorials, pronunciation guides, and cultural insights.

3. Language Exchange Programs:

Immersing yourself in the local culture is a proven method of language acquisition. Language exchange programs, such as Tandem and ConversationExchange, connect language learners with native Slovenian speakers. Through these platforms, you can engage in language exchanges, either in person or online, where you practice Slovenian while helping your language partner learn your native tongue. This reciprocal learning experience fosters friendships, cultural understanding, and rapid language development.

4. Language Apps:

For those constantly on the go, language learning apps offer a convenient way to study Slovenian anytime, anywhere. Apps like HelloTalk, Tandem, and HiNative connect language learners with native speakers through text, voice, and video chats. These platforms provide an opportunity to practice conversational skills, receive real-time corrections, and ask questions about the language. Additionally, apps like Anki and Quizlet offer flashcards and spaced repetition techniques to enhance vocabulary retention.

5. Language Immersion Programs:

To accelerate your language learning journey, consider participating in a language immersion program in Slovenia. These programs offer a full immersion experience, where you live with a host family, attend language classes, and engage in cultural activities. The intensive nature of these programs allows for rapid language acquisition and a deeper understanding of Slovenian customs and traditions. Some renowned language immersion programs in Slovenia include the Summer School of Slovene Language, the Slovenian Language School in Maribor, and the Slovenian Cultural Summer School.

Conclusion:

Learning the language of Slovenia opens doors to a deeper connection with the country and its people. Whether you choose to enroll in language schools, explore online resources, participate in language exchange programs, or immerse yourself in language immersion programs, the resources available are abundant. Embrace the opportunity to learn Slovenian, and you will undoubtedly enhance your travel experience, build lasting relationships, and gain a profound appreciation for the rich culture and heritage of Slovenia.

Chapter 39: Tips for Traveling with Children in Slovenia

Introduction:

Traveling with children can be an exciting and rewarding experience, especially when visiting a country as beautiful and family-friendly as Slovenia. With its stunning landscapes, rich culture, and numerous attractions, Slovenia offers a wealth of opportunities for families to create lasting memories. This chapter aims to provide you with valuable tips and advice on how to make the most of your family vacation in Slovenia, ensuring a smooth and enjoyable journey for everyone.

What to Pack:

1. Clothing: Slovenia experiences a variety of climates, so it is essential to pack clothes suitable for different weather conditions. Be sure to include comfortable walking shoes, raincoats, and layers that can be easily added or removed.

2. Snacks and Entertainment: To keep your children entertained during long journeys or while waiting for attractions, pack their favorite snacks, books, coloring materials, and travel games. Having familiar items on hand can help keep them occupied and content.

3. Medications and First Aid Kit: It is always wise to bring any necessary medications your children may require, along with a basic first aid kit. This ensures you are prepared for any minor injuries or illnesses that may occur during your trip.

Accommodation:

1. Family-Friendly Hotels: When choosing accommodation, opt for family-friendly hotels that offer amenities such as play areas, swimming pools, and babysitting services. Many hotels in Slovenia cater specifically to families, ensuring a comfortable stay for all.

2. Self-Catering Accommodations: Consider booking self-catering accommodations, such as apartments or holiday homes, which provide a kitchenette or full kitchen. This allows you to prepare meals for your children according to their preferences and dietary needs, saving both time and money.

3. Location: Select accommodations that are centrally located or in close proximity to attractions, parks, and public transportation. This will minimize travel time and make it easier to explore Slovenia with your little ones.

Things to Do:

1. Visit Ljubljana Zoo: A visit to the Ljubljana Zoo is a must for families traveling with children. This well-maintained zoo is home to a wide variety of animals and offers educational programs and interactive exhibits that will captivate young minds.

2. Explore Postojna Cave: Take your children on an unforgettable adventure through the magical Postojna Cave. This extensive underground network of caves is accessible by train and provides a mesmerizing experience for both children and adults.

3. Discover Lake Bled: Lake Bled is a picture-perfect destination that offers a range of family-friendly activities. Rent a rowboat or take a traditional pletna boat ride to the island in the middle of the lake, where you can explore the charming church and ring the wishing bell.

4. Experience Triglav National Park: For families who love outdoor adventures, a visit to Triglav National Park is a must. Enjoy hiking, cycling, or even horseback riding amidst breathtaking landscapes, ensuring a memorable experience for the whole family.

Conclusion:

Traveling with children in Slovenia can be an enriching and enjoyable experience for the entire family. By following the tips provided in this chapter, you can ensure a smooth and stress-free journey, creating lasting memories that your children will cherish. From packing wisely to choosing family-friendly accommodations and engaging in exciting activities, Slovenia offers a plethora of opportunities for family fun and exploration. So, embrace the beauty of Slovenia and embark on an unforgettable adventure with your little ones.

Chapter 40: Tips for Traveling with Seniors in Slovenia

Traveling with seniors can be a rewarding and enriching experience, especially when exploring the beautiful country of Slovenia. With its stunning landscapes, rich history, and warm hospitality, Slovenia offers a plethora of opportunities for seniors to enjoy. To ensure a smooth and enjoyable trip for both you and your senior companions, here are some valuable tips to consider.

1. Prioritize Comfortable Accommodation:

When selecting accommodation, prioritize comfort and convenience. Look for hotels or rental properties that offer accessible rooms, elevators, and amenities that cater to the needs of seniors. Opt for central locations to minimize walking distances and ensure easy access to public transportation.

2. Pack Essentials and Medications:

Before embarking on your trip, make a checklist of essential items and medications your seniors may require. Pack comfortable clothing suitable for the weather, sturdy walking shoes, and any necessary medical supplies. It's also advisable to carry a copy of their medical records, prescriptions, and emergency contact information.

3. Plan for Adequate Rest and Breaks:

Seniors may require more rest and breaks during the day. Plan your itinerary accordingly, allowing for ample time to relax and recharge. Avoid overpacking the schedule and be flexible with plans to accommodate their needs and energy levels.

4. Opt for Guided Tours:

Consider booking guided tours or hiring local guides to explore Slovenia's attractions. This ensures that seniors can enjoy the sights and learn about the country's history without feeling overwhelmed or fatigued. Guides can also provide valuable insights and assistance along the way.

5. Choose Accessible Attractions:

Slovenia offers a variety of attractions suitable for seniors. Opt for places that are easily accessible and have amenities such as ramps, elevators, and benches. Explore charming towns like Ljubljana, Bled, and Piran, where seniors can stroll along picturesque streets, visit cafes, and enjoy the local culture at a leisurely pace.

6. Embrace Nature's Beauty:

Slovenia is renowned for its breathtaking natural landscapes. Take advantage of the country's well-maintained hiking trails, parks, and lakes. Encourage seniors to enjoy gentle walks amidst stunning scenery, such as Lake Bohinj, Triglav National Park, or the Postojna Cave. Remember to pack a picnic to savor the beauty of nature while enjoying a relaxing break.

7. Utilize Public Transportation:

Slovenia has an efficient and reliable public transportation system, making it easy to navigate the country. Utilize buses and trains, which often offer senior discounts, to minimize walking distances and provide a comfortable mode of transportation. Be sure to plan your routes in advance and check for any accessibility options.

8. Indulge in Local Cuisine:

Slovenian cuisine is diverse and delicious, offering a range of dishes to satisfy different palates. Encourage seniors to try traditional Slovenian delicacies such as potica (rolled pastry), štruklji (rolled dumplings), or Kranjska klobasa (Carniolan sausage). Ensure that dietary restrictions or preferences are taken into account when dining out.

9. Stay Hydrated and Mindful of Health:

Remind seniors to stay hydrated throughout the trip, especially during warmer months. Carry a water bottle and encourage regular hydration breaks. Additionally, be mindful of their health by avoiding strenuous activities, providing shade or sun protection, and being aware of any potential allergies or medical conditions.

10. Embrace the Slovenian Hospitality:

Slovenians are known for their warm hospitality and friendliness. Encourage seniors to interact with locals, who are often more than willing to assist and offer helpful advice. Engaging with the local culture and people can enhance the overall travel experience, creating lasting memories.

By considering these tips, you can ensure a memorable and enjoyable trip while traveling with seniors in Slovenia. Remember to prioritize their comfort, health, and interests to create an enriching experience for all. Happy travels!

Chapter 41: Tips for Traveling Solo in Slovenia

Traveling solo can be an incredibly rewarding experience, allowing you the freedom to explore at your own pace and immerse yourself in the local culture. Slovenia, with its stunning landscapes, rich history, and warm hospitality, is an ideal destination for solo travelers. In this chapter, we will provide you with valuable tips to make your solo adventure in Slovenia unforgettable, safe, and enjoyable.

Where to Stay:

1. Hostels: Slovenia offers a wide range of hostels that cater to solo travelers, providing affordable accommodation and a chance to meet fellow adventurers.

2. Guesthouses: Stay in cozy guesthouses run by friendly locals, where you can experience the warm Slovenian hospitality and get insider tips on the best places to visit.

3. Couchsurfing: Consider Couchsurfing, a platform that connects travelers with locals willing to offer a free place to stay. This is a great opportunity to meet Slovenian residents and gain a deeper understanding of the country.

Things to Do:

1. Explore Ljubljana: Start your solo journey in the charming capital city of Ljubljana. Wander through the picturesque old town, visit the iconic Ljubljana Castle, and enjoy the vibrant café culture along the Ljubljanica River.

2. Discover Lake Bled: A must-visit destination in Slovenia, Lake Bled offers breathtaking scenery. Take a solo hike around the lake, visit Bled Castle, and don't miss the chance to row out to the island and ring the famous Wishing Bell.

3. Embrace Nature in Triglav National Park: Slovenia's only national park is a paradise for outdoor enthusiasts. Hike through the

Julian Alps, explore the emerald-green Soča River, and challenge yourself with a solo climb to the summit of Mount Triglav, the country's highest peak.

Staying Safe:

1. Inform Others: Before embarking on your solo adventure, inform a trusted friend or family member about your travel plans, including your itinerary and accommodation details.

2. Stay Connected: Ensure you have a reliable means of communication, such as a local SIM card or an international roaming plan, to stay connected with emergency services and loved ones.

3. Trust Your Instincts: While Slovenia is generally a safe country, it's important to trust your instincts and be cautious, especially when venturing into unfamiliar areas or at night. Avoid isolated areas and be aware of your surroundings.

4. Secure Your Belongings: Keep your personal belongings secure by using a lockable bag or a money belt. Be cautious of pickpockets in crowded tourist areas and public transportation.

Remember, solo travel in Slovenia offers endless opportunities for self-discovery and adventure. By following these tips, you'll be well-prepared to make the most of your solo journey, ensuring a safe and memorable experience in this enchanting country.

Chapter 42: Tips for Traveling on a Budget in Slovenia

Introduction:

Welcome to Slovenia, a stunning country nestled in the heart of Europe. Known for its breathtaking landscapes, charming cities, and warm hospitality, Slovenia offers a plethora of experiences for travelers on a budget. In this chapter, we will provide you with valuable tips on how to make the most of your trip while keeping your expenses in check. From affordable accommodation options to budget-friendly activities, we've got you covered.

1. Choosing Budget-Friendly Accommodation:

When it comes to finding affordable places to stay in Slovenia, consider the following options:

- Hostels: Slovenia boasts numerous hostels that offer comfortable and affordable accommodations, perfect for budget-conscious travelers. Ljubljana, the capital city, is known for its excellent hostel scene.

- Guesthouses: Opting for guesthouses or private rooms in local homes is not only cost-effective but also a great way to immerse yourself in Slovenian culture. Websites like Airbnb and Booking.com offer a wide range of choices.

- Campsites: If you enjoy outdoor adventures, Slovenia offers an abundance of campsites, allowing you to experience the country's natural beauty while saving money.

2. Exploring Affordable Destinations:

While Slovenia is relatively small, it offers diverse landscapes and attractions. Here are some budget-friendly destinations to consider:

- Ljubljana: The capital city is not only charming but also offers numerous free attractions, including exploring the historic Old Town, visiting the Ljubljana Castle, and strolling along the Ljubljanica River.

- Lake Bled: This iconic destination is a must-visit in Slovenia. Enjoy the stunning lake, hike to the Bled Castle, and take a walk around the lake's perimeter without spending a fortune.

- Triglav National Park: Nature enthusiasts will find solace in this breathtaking national park. Hiking trails, waterfalls, and serene landscapes await, providing an affordable escape into nature.

3. Enjoying Budget-Friendly Activities:

Slovenia offers a range of activities that won't break the bank. Here are a few suggestions:

- Free Walking Tours: Many cities, including Ljubljana, offer free walking tours led by knowledgeable guides. Explore the city's highlights while learning about its history and culture.

- Picnics in Nature: Take advantage of Slovenia's beautiful landscapes and pack a picnic. Enjoy a meal surrounded by stunning scenery, whether it's by Lake Bohinj, the Soča River, or the vineyards of the Vipava Valley.

- Local Markets: Immerse yourself in the local culture by visiting bustling markets. From fresh produce to handcrafted souvenirs, you can find unique items at reasonable prices.

4. Dining on a Budget:

While exploring Slovenia, you can savor delicious meals without overspending. Consider these tips:

- Local Eateries: Opt for small local restaurants and bistros that offer authentic Slovenian cuisine at affordable prices. Ask locals for recommendations to discover hidden gems.

- Street Food: Grab a quick bite from street food stalls, where you can find traditional snacks such as burek (pastry filled with cheese or meat) or kranjska klobasa (Carniolan sausage).

- Self-Catering: If you're staying in accommodation with kitchen facilities, take advantage of local supermarkets and farmers' markets to cook your meals. This allows you to experience local ingredients and save money.

Conclusion:

Traveling on a budget in Slovenia is entirely possible with careful planning and these tips in mind. From selecting affordable accommodations to exploring budget-friendly destinations and activities, you can experience the wonders of Slovenia without breaking the bank. Remember, the true essence of travel lies in embracing the local culture and immersing yourself in the beauty of your surroundings. So, pack your bags, embark on a budget-friendly adventure, and create unforgettable memories in Slovenia.

Chapter 43: Tips for Traveling Responsibly in Slovenia

Introduction:

As a responsible traveler, it is essential to minimize your impact on the environment and culture of the places you visit. Slovenia, with its breathtaking landscapes, rich cultural heritage, and warm hospitality, offers an ideal setting to practice sustainable and responsible tourism. In this chapter, we will provide you with valuable tips on how to travel responsibly in Slovenia, ensuring that you leave only footprints and take away unforgettable memories.

1. Respect the Environment:

Slovenia is renowned for its pristine nature, from the picturesque Julian Alps to the enchanting Lake Bled. To minimize your impact on the environment:

a. Stick to designated trails and paths when hiking or exploring nature reserves to avoid damaging fragile ecosystems.

b. Dispose of waste responsibly by using designated bins or taking it with you until you find a suitable disposal point.

c. Opt for eco-friendly transportation options like cycling or using public transport whenever possible to reduce carbon emissions.

d. Conserve water by taking shorter showers and reusing towels in accommodations that promote sustainable practices.

2. Embrace Local Culture:

Slovenia boasts a rich cultural heritage, influenced by its diverse history and neighboring countries. To respect and immerse yourself in the local culture:

a. Learn a few basic Slovenian phrases to communicate with locals, showing your interest and respect for their language.

b. Familiarize yourself with local customs and traditions, such as removing your shoes before entering someone's home or covering your shoulders when visiting religious sites.

c. Support local artisans and businesses by purchasing authentic Slovenian handicrafts and products, contributing directly to the local economy.

d. Engage in cultural activities and events, such as traditional festivals or folk dances, to gain a deeper understanding of Slovenia's cultural identity.

3. Choose Sustainable Accommodations:

When selecting accommodations in Slovenia, prioritize establishments that prioritize sustainability and responsible practices:

a. Look for eco-certifications such as the EU Ecolabel or Green Key, ensuring that the accommodation meets specific environmental standards.

b. Stay in locally-owned accommodations, such as family-run guesthouses or eco-friendly farms, to support the local community.

c. Conserve energy by turning off lights and air conditioning when not in use, and consider reusing towels and bed linen to reduce water and energy consumption.

d. Opt for accommodations that serve locally-sourced and organic food, supporting sustainable agriculture and reducing the carbon footprint associated with food transportation.

4. Engage in Responsible Outdoor Activities:

Slovenia's natural beauty offers numerous opportunities for outdoor activities. Ensure you enjoy these activities responsibly:

a. Choose licensed and responsible tour operators for activities like kayaking, canyoning, or paragliding, ensuring they adhere to safety and environmental regulations.

b. Respect wildlife and refrain from feeding or disturbing animals in their natural habitats.

c. Practice Leave No Trace principles by packing out any trash or waste generated during outdoor activities.

d. Consider joining volunteer programs or eco-tourism initiatives that contribute to the conservation and preservation of Slovenia's natural areas.

Conclusion:

By following these tips for traveling responsibly in Slovenia, you will not only have an unforgettable experience but also contribute positively to the preservation of Slovenia's environment and culture. Remember, responsible tourism is not just about the places we visit, but the impact we leave behind for future generations to enjoy.